Needlework

THE SMITHSONIAN ILLUSTRATED LIBRARY OF ANTIQUES

General Editor: Brenda Gilchrist

Needlework

Adolph S. Cavallo

COOPER-HEWITT MUSEUM

The Smithsonian Institution's National Museum of Design

ENDPAPERS
Detail of a pattern for needlework from Thomas Trevelyon's *Miscellany* manuscript of 1608, folio 239. Folger Shakespeare Library, Washington, D.C.

FRONTISPIECE
The goddess Flora, as pictured in this wall hanging representing Spring, is believed to portray Mademoiselle de Blois, one of the daughters of Louis XIV and Madame de Montespan. The hanging was probably worked by girls trained by the nuns in the Convent of St. Joseph de la Providence in Paris. French, about 1683. Height: 417 cm. (164 in.). Detail. Metropolitan Museum of Art, New York, Rogers Fund, 1946

This book is dedicated to Alice Baldwin Beer, Curator Emeritus, Textiles Department, Cooper-Hewitt Museum

Art Direction, Design: JOSEPH B. DEL VALLE

Text Editor: JOAN HOFFMAN

Picture Editor: LISA LITTLE

Contents

1   Introduction

The art of needlework must be as old as civilization itself. As primeval man developed, he looked for ways to extend the capabilities of his body. He looked for weapons and tools and found them ready-made in nature. A tree limb or heavy bone could fell food on the hoof better than a pair of hands. He looked for materials to clothe himself, and found these in nature too. Thick pelts cut from the backs of furbearing animals with a sharp stone or shell could warm a human body far better than its own miserly covering of hair. A splinter of bone or a thorn could pierce those pelts, and then stout grasses or gut could be pulled through the holes to tie the pelts together. Needlework in its simplest form was born.

This book, however, is not about beginnings but about a later period in world history, a time in the relatively recent past when men and women engaged in needlework as an art form rather than as a utilitarian necessity. It attempts to give the general reader a general introduction to its subject, and like all general introductions to very specific subjects, it is incomplete. Although it spans two thousand years of the practice of decorative needlework in different parts of the world, it does not encompass needlework everywhere in the world or over the entire period. Not enough is known about the subject to attempt a comprehensive survey, but in any case such an undertaking would require many volumes the size of this to tell the full story.

Nevertheless, if *Needlework* can help the reader understand what decorative needlework has been (at least in some cultures, at some times) and how needlework relates to the history of art in general, and how to go about developing a critical eye for attributions and quality, then its purpose will have been served. With this goal in mind the author has illustrated extraordinary examples of needlework art when he thought they could set standards for judging quality; otherwise, the examples are typical rather than exceptional, and show

Colorplate 1.
This elegant American sampler proclaims: "Mary Batchelder Was Born June The 13th 1757 Wrought this Sampler 1773. While God Does Spare For Death Prepare." Height: 41 cm. (16⅛ in.). Cooper-Hewitt Museum, bequest of Mrs. Henry E. Coe, 1941

1.
Der Seidensticker (The Silk Embroiderer). A professional silk embroiderer at his trade. Typically, the foundation fabric is stretched on a frame, in this case a rectangular one. Woodcut illustration from a German book, 1550–1600. Cooper-Hewitt Museum, gift of the Estate of Mrs. Lathrop Colgate Harper, 1957

things of a kind most readily found in public collections and markets. Many of the pieces illustrated are from the Cooper-Hewitt Museum's own remarkable collection, which represents a broad range of needlework art.

Confronted with the mass of embroideries surviving from the past, the beginning collector or student of needlework stands in danger of drowning in the seemingly boundless sea of miscellaneous material, thus losing sight of the people and purposes that generated these works of art. Getting to know the who, why and how of historical needlework is half the fun of working with old embroideries. It is important therefore in these opening pages to isolate and examine certain basic questions, questions whose answers will help focus the beginner's attention as he sets out to find enlightenment and enjoyment. Who were the people who practiced needlework? What were their motives? Where did they get their training and how did they get their patterns? Why, of all the crafts, does needlework seem so very familiar, so homely, so easily approachable?

The answer to the last question is simple. Needlework is just one step away from drawing; and drawing is simply the act of recording the eye's perceptions through movements of the hand. It is this immediacy, this intimate connection with the human body, that gives needlework its universal appeal; and because the craft can be practiced at home with minimal capital and equipment, it is essentially different from all the others.

Crafts like porcelain making, goldsmithing, furniture making and clockmaking are, and always have been, practiced primarily as economically viable industries, although in the past, as now, a few people working as individuals have successfully made bowls, jewelry, chairs and the like for gain or pleasure or both. But both groups of people have had to deal with problems of obtaining capital, special equipment and space, and usually they have also had to spend years either developing their native talents or acquiring skills that did not come naturally to them. Because of all this, not everyone can practice these crafts.

Needlework, as we have said, is a very different matter. Today anyone can practice needlework, and in the past just about anyone did—anyone, that is, who could afford to make or buy the few necessary materials, who could find a comfortable corner to work in, and who could also spend the money to buy or rent patterns or had the time to learn them free from someone else.

During past centuries, whether the needleworker was the wife of the humblest shepherd on an island in the Aegean Sea or a queen at Versailles, every third woman in the world—this is just an estimate, but a fair one—took up her needle, thread and cloth to decorate a garment or household object for herself, her home or her brood. Other women, and men, used needlework skills as a way of earning income. Others, lucky enough to have leisure time, worked with a needle for diversion, as a hobby. Still other people of both sexes worked silks, linens, wools, precious metals and gems for the greater glory of God; these were the nuns and monks whose concern for economic gain from their needlework ranked close to zero on the motivation scale.

All these people—whether housewives, girls anticipating the pleasures of womanhood, royal women ruling great courts (and their unacknowledged rivals, the royal mistresses), men or orphan girls earning a living, people in convents or today's tense, harried businessmen—all these have contributed to the growth and glory of one of the greatest arts that man's mind has ever conceived: the art of needlework.

Because we so often use the word *art* in connection with the needlework that has come down to us over the generations, we mistake skill (one meaning of *art*) for creative ability (another level of the meaning of *art*) and assume, quite incorrectly, that most or all needleworkers of the past designed their own patterns and chose their own colors, just as painters and draftsmen designed their own compositions. That is simply not so. Overwhelming evidence indicates that while some men and women worked textiles after their own patterns and choices of color and material, the vast majority of needleworkers

2.
The women in this embroidery workshop are professional needleworkers producing embroidered fronts for men's waistcoats. The frames used in such industrial settings were generally much larger than those used by home workers. Engraving from the *Encyclopédie, ou dictionnaire universel des arts et des sciences*. French, 1762–65. Cooper-Hewitt Museum, 1949

3.
On this curtain for the ark in which the Torah is kept in a synagogue, a female professional needleworker has represented the Tablets of the Law, Mount Sinai and the walled city of Jerusalem. Italian, signed by Simha, wife of Menahem Levy Meshullami, and dated 1680–81. Height: 216 cm. (85 in.). Jewish Museum, New York, gift of Professor Neppi Modona, Florence, through Dr. Harry G. Friedman, 1952

used standard patterns created by specialized designers and made available to anyone who could afford them—exactly as happens today. The notion that schoolgirls, young housewives, nuns and monks embroidered flowers or saints after their own patterns is charming, but it is a charming myth.

The men and women who worked the textiles discussed and illustrated in this book were for the most part people like the rest of us. Except for a few pieces made by enormously skilled male and female professional needleworkers, the works come from the hands of women who were as adept at making bread, managing a household or spanking children as they were at handling their needles.

Throughout its long history, literally millions of ordinary people have practiced needlework, and their work remains entirely anonymous. Still, a few initials and names worked into embroideries have transmitted to us the names of some domestic workers and nuns who signed their work out of a sense of devotion and pride. Professional needleworkers, at least in Western Europe, also sometimes signed their work.

In Western Europe, thousands of men and women earned their livelihood at needlework, as we know from the many signatures, documents and pictorial representations left to us (plate 1). Like other European professional craftsmen, needleworkers formed guilds sometime in the early Middle Ages. Primarily, members of a guild banded together to control the training of apprentices, to maintain standards of workmanship and to establish funds for members in need, but they also usually lived together in a particular part of a town or city and mingled socially as well as at work. Records of the early years of the needlework guilds are scarce, and research in this field is still in its infancy, but we know, for example, that the Broderers' Company of London was chartered in 1561 and that an even earlier London guild for embroiderers existed. We know, too, that in the silk guild of Florence in the fourteenth century, professional embroiderers constituted a separate body, as did the makers of ecclesiastical vestments. We have the names of two great Florentine embroiderers of that period: Jacopo Campi, who in 1336 signed and dated an embroidered altar frontal (now in the Museo degli Argenti in Florence), and Geri Lapi, who signed but did not date a similar altar hanging (now in the Church of Santa María in Manresa, Spain).

We also have the names of a few female needleworkers, among them Simha Meshullami, who signed and dated a curtain for a Torah ark in the late seventeenth century in Italy (plate 3). We can assume that relatively large numbers of women made a living at needlework during the seventeenth and eighteenth centuries both because they are shown at the work in contemporary illustrations (plate 2) and also because we know that young girls were trained at that time as needleworkers in convents and charitable institutions. One of these was the home for impoverished girls run by the nuns of the Convent of St. Joseph de la Providence in Paris. During the last quarter of the seventeenth century the convent was patronized by Madame de Montespan, mistress of Louis XIV, and under her patronage the home became famous for the varied and exquisite needlework of its young charges (see frontispiece).

Nuns in convents practiced needlework much earlier than this, and a great deal of their work, some of it signed, has survived from the Middle Ages. In the Metropolitan Museum of Art in New York, for example, is an early fourteenth-century linen altar cloth from the convent of Altenburg in Germany signed by Sophia, Hadewigis and Lucardis, who are believed to have been nuns there. The same museum has a somewhat later hanging, also German and also thought to have been worked by nuns (colorplate 5, see page 42). Convent work like this stands on middle ground between the work of professional embroiderers, such as Jacopo Campi, Edmund Harrison (embroiderer to James I, Charles I and Charles II of England) and Simha Meshullami, and the incalculably larger number of amateur embroideries that have come to us from the hands of millions upon millions of women who practiced needlework as a domestic art.

In rural societies, women learned the methods and materials of needlework from their elders, and traditions were handed down from generation to generation. Rural women learned to embroider so they could make essential house furnishings and clothes, especially their dowry clothes and decorations. Fashions penetrated slowly into provincial regions, and consequently old patterns and procedures remained in favor there longer than they did in cities.

In cities, the ability to embroider was admired in a high-born woman, whether she was royal or noble or a rich commoner. Queens and women of high position, including Elizabeth I of England, Mary Queen of Scots and Madame de Maintenon, last influential mistress of Louis XIV, were accomplished needlewomen themselves or had about them ladies-in-waiting who were expert embroiderers, or they patronized professional embroiderers. Women of these ranks learned needlework either from professional embroiderers or in schools established to train young women in ladylike graces. In the eighteenth and nineteenth centuries schools like these flourished even in the relatively new communities prospering in the North American colonies.

One of the earliest recorded American schools was kept in Boston for a few years beginning in 1712 by George Brownell, who taught writing, arithmetic and needlework—necessary graces for young women. A few years later George and Bridget Suckling taught the same subjects in their school, also in Boston. About the same time, around 1740–50, a Mrs. Condy was selling needlework materials and patterns and also teaching in Boston. A Mrs. Carroll taught needlework in New York in 1765, and the next year a needlework teacher named E. Gardner placed an advertisement in a Virginia newspaper announcing similar instruction. In Pennsylvania there were schools kept by the Moravians and Quakers, as well as private schools, where from the middle of the eighteenth century until well into the next girls were taught both simple and fine needlework. Miss Polly Balch's Seminary in Providence, Rhode Island, taught needlework to girls from the late eighteenth century to the early nineteenth.

Samplers worked by girls in these schools (or at home) served not only as examples of their current work but as pattern sources for future work. As we have seen, most needleworkers did not make up their own designs, and samplers were sources of patterns for hundreds of years. Indeed, in England during the sixteenth century samplers were kept in families for generations, not out of sentiment but because of their value as a source of patterns and stitches. After about 1700 they were made primarily as part of a girl's training in needlework and to demonstrate her growing proficiency. Representations of numerals and letters figure prominently in the samplers worked by young girls since as housewives, after they grew up and were married, they would be responsible for the marking of dates and initials on their family's household and personal linen (sheets, petticoats, chemises, etc.).

Varying in shape, size and pattern, depending on the date and place of working, samplers are found in the needlework of many cultures, including that of ancient Peru. But the samplers most familiar to modern eyes are those worked in Europe or America during the period from the seventeenth to the nineteenth century (plates 4 and 5; colorplate 1).

Although a few seventeenth-century samplers from New England have survived, we have many more that were worked in England, which provided the models for the colonial pieces. At present, the earliest dated English sampler known to us is the one worked by Jane Bostocke in 1598 that is now in the Victoria and Albert Museum in London. The long, narrow sampler in plate 4 demonstrates the typical shape of English pieces of the seventeenth century, although squarer samplers were also made then. Some samplers show only openwork and lace stitches; others, like the example in plate 4, retain their solid linen foundation and display a variety of ornamental stitches, especially cross, satin, eyelet, couching and stem stitches. (Illustrations of some of the stitches most commonly found in historical needlework appear on page 120. For illustrations and discussions of stitches not included there, the author suggests that the reader see the three volumes listed under "Technical" in the Reading and Reference section on page 124.)

While the assortment of stitches varies from sampler to sampler, most seventeenth-century English and American colonial pieces exhibit the same kinds of patterns: flowers, the alphabet, an inscription (generally a pious verse), numerals and, usually, the maker's name and

4.
The inscription on this English sampler reads: "Sarah Barrett made this sampler in the eight year of her age 1678." Spelling errors like "eight" for "eighth" were common even in samplers of older needleworkers. Height: 82.5 cm. (32½ in.). Cooper-Hewitt Museum, bequest of Mrs. Henry E. Coe, 1941

the date. A hundred years later the formula had changed very little: neither the choice of stitches nor the pattern is much different, although most of the linen foundations of the later period have a more nearly square shape (colorplate 1). Some of the dates prove that girls as young as seven or eight were at work on these sample pieces. When we take into account the early ages at which people married and died at the time, this discovery seems less surprising than it might.

Samplers worked in the various American colonies in the eighteenth century tend to show regional differences because certain patterns persisted in certain schools. For example, students in Polly Balch's school in Providence worked representations in their samplers of such local structures as the old State House, University Hall at Brown University and the First Baptist Meeting House. Local and national traditions account for the major differences between American samplers and those worked on the continent of Europe during this period. German eighteenth-century samplers, for instance, often contain not only the floral forms and alphabets common in American samplers but also many human figures, some of them biblical (plate 5). And Continental samplers frequently show symbols of the Virgin and symbols referring to the Passion of Christ.

Both amateur and professional embroiderers used engravings and illustrated books, especially the Bible, as sources for their patterns. There were also printed sources intended specifically for the use of needleworkers, such as the books containing patterns for both lace and needlework that were published in Italy, Germany and other Continental nations in the sixteenth and seventeenth centuries. Today we can occasionally match up an existing piece of needlework with the pattern from which it was worked (plates 6 and 7).

A number of pattern books were also published in England. Many of these were based on the Continental models, but at least one of them, Richard Shorleyker's *A Schole-house for the needle . . .* (1624 and later editions), contains some original motifs. As we will see in the next chapter, English domestic needlework of the sixteenth and seventeenth centuries had a design character all its own. Patterns with this distinctive character appear in two design manuscripts prepared by an English penman named Thomas Trevelyon, one dating from 1608, the other from 1616. Although some of the patterns may have been intended to serve as models for woodcarvers or workers in decorative plaster, or for wallpaper printers, as well as for embroiderers, others clearly were meant for embroiderers alone (plate 8). Some of the textiles worked from patterns similar to Trevelyon's display colored silks and gilt and silver yarns; others, showing only black silk on white foundations, look much more like his black-and-white illustrations (plate 9).

Other patterns worked at this time were derived from illustrated books dealing with plants and animals. Still others, chiefly those with

5.
Some of the motifs in this German sampler dated 1753 were taken from Johann Sibmacher's widely reprinted pattern book *Newes Modelbuch*, which was first published in Nuremberg about 1600. Height: 110.5 cm. (43½ in.). Metropolitan Museum of Art, New York, gift of Margaret Taylor Johnston, 1908

pictorial subjects rather than simple ornamental motifs, were adapted from loose prints or prints bound into books. Thanks to recent research, we can now trace a number of surviving European embroideries (as well as printed and tapestry-woven fabrics) back to their printed sources (plates 10 and 11).

Needleworkers resorted to different means to get the patterns in books transformed into patterns ready for their needles. Most domestic workers employed professional pattern drawers to prepare the patterns for them. Professional needleworkers probably had the skill to adapt the designs themselves and then draw out the patterns on the foundation fabrics. But the professionals would sometimes call on the services of contemporary painters in their search for patterns for pictorial needlework. The earliest documentary evidence we have of this practice lies in an early fifteenth-century treatise on painting by Cennino Cennini, a pupil of the great fourteenth-century Florentine painter Agnolo Gaddi, that includes instructions for drawing patterns directly on fabric. Although Cennini did not write his treatise until the fifteenth century, he incorporates references to procedures of the previous century as well, indicating that artists were drawing patterns for embroiderers at least as early as the fourteenth century.

There were also professional designers of ornamental needlework, but we know very little about them. Mary Queen of Scots employed at least one embroiderer "to drawe forthe such worke as she would be occupied about." Many pattern drawers, writing masters and needleworkers offered a similar service through advertisements in colonial American newspapers during the eighteenth century. Great commercial embroidery firms like that of St. Ruf in France, which thrived in the last part of the eighteenth century, employed both designers of needlework and needleworkers themselves. While the

6.
In this detail of the border of a table cover worked with red silk, Cupid aims his arrow at a female victim. The design was taken from the printed pattern shown in plate 7. Italian, 1560–1600. Height of border: about 10.2 cm. (4 in.). Cooper-Hewitt Museum, bequest of Marian Hague, 1971

7.
This is the Cupid detail from the printed pattern after which the piece in plate 6 was worked. The pattern appeared in Mathio Pagan's *La gloria et l'honore de ponti tagliati e ponti in aere*, an early pattern book for lacemakers and embroiderers published in Venice in 1558. Reproduced from *Quaritch's Reprints of Rare Books* (London, 1884). Cooper-Hewitt Museum

8.
Thomas Trevelyon, whose two design manuscripts have left us a record of many of the English needlework patterns of the early seventeenth century, provided this pattern for a man's needlework cap and its border. This kind of cap is typical of the headgear English gentlemen wore at home to complete a fine costume. From Trevelyon's *Miscellany* manuscript of 1608, folio 270 verso. Detail. Folger Shakespeare Library, Washington, D.C.

6

7

names of the workers are consistently those of women, the names of the designers are of both men and women. Their patterns, drawn in black and white or painted in color, were intended specifically for needlework on garments (colorplate 2).

Simpler patterns drawn out in pencil or ink on paper were widely used. During the nineteenth century such patterns were collected by professional needleworkers and by women for their own domestic work (plate 14). They were probably copied or adapted from the popular patterns published in *Godey's Lady's Book, Peterson's Magazine* and other ladies' magazines throughout most of the nineteenth century.

The business of publishing patterns for domestic needleworkers got a great and sudden boost early in the nineteenth century with the rise of the rage for Berlin work (plates 12 and 13). The first patterns were published in Germany and later imitated elsewhere in Europe and in America. The technique of Berlin work will be discussed fully later on. Suffice it for now to say that the method was that of counted-thread work on canvas.

Still another source of needlework patterns were textiles themselves. Professional embroiderers took inspiration from rich silks woven in the great textile centers in Italy, France and elsewhere, and some domestic workers probably did the same. Perhaps some of these textile patterns were also available in published form. We know, for example, that embroideries worked in India and China in the seventeenth and eighteenth centuries for the Western market were designed after models sent from Europe, particularly from England and Portugal. And in one case, the same pattern was executed in two different techniques in India (plates 15 and 16) and in yet a third technique in England (plate 17). Did the English needleworker copy the two

8

9

9.
Worked solely with black silk yarns, this cushion cover reflects the English love of garden plants like columbines and strawberries. English, probably 1600–1610. Length: 91 cm. (36 in.). Detail. Cooper-Hewitt Museum, purchase, Au Panier Fleuri Fund, 1956

10

11

Indian examples after they reached Europe, or did all three craftsmen have access to the same published source? We can only guess.

This question touches on the matter of stylistic development in the art of needlework, a subject of particular importance when one examines the place of needlework in the main tradition of art in the West. Although the decorative arts, of which needlework is one, involve ornamental elements rather than pictorial compositions, their development, like that of painting, sculpture and architecture, exhibits certain evolving ways of composing forms in space and of rendering the forms themselves. These changing attitudes toward composition, drawing, color and scale define the style of a period or culture. In this sense, style means neither fashion nor stylishness, nor does it refer to a specific set of ornaments. Rather, style in this context concerns the major artistic attitudes of any culture, attitudes that cut across the boundaries of mediums and nations and during a given period produce music in Germany, plays in France and pictures in Italy that share the same feeling of movement or stability, simplicity or complexity, clarity or obscurity—the same *period style*. This is a subtle idea, and one particularly difficult to isolate and examine when

10.
Moses Parting the Two Quarreling Hebrews (left) and *Moses with the Daughters of the Priest of Midian* (right). These woodcut illustrations by Bernard Salomon for the *Quadrins historiques de la bible* published in Lyons in 1553 are the pattern source for the figures shown in plate 11. Museum of Fine Arts, Boston, bequest of W. G. Russell Allen, 1964

11.
For this tent-stitched valance based on the biblical woodcuts in plate 10, the needlework designer reworked the landscape setting as a proper background for the figures. Probably French, about 1600. Height: 44.5 cm. (17½ in.). Metropolitan Museum of Art, New York, gift of Irwin Untermyer, 1953

dealing with needlework, metalwork, ceramics or any of the decorative arts because the particular character of the ornaments interferes with one's perception of their rendering and arrangement.

Three needlework examples, chosen from three major periods in the history of Western art and illustrated alongside examples of other kinds of objects from the same periods, will help us visualize this concept of period style. The first example, from the Renaissance, is a strip of needlework that was worked in Italy or Spain about 1525–50 (plate 18). It has a scrolling vine pattern that for all its curves and twistings remains symmetrical, static, clear. The double-ended unit repeats clearly end to end, and is neatly contained within the width of the strip. A similar choice of ornaments, more elaborate and varied but equally clear and equally well contained within the space provided for them by the paneling system, appears in an example of woodcarving from Italy dating from the same period (plate 19). Still another similar set of ornaments neatly fills the space of a border painted on the surface of an earthenware dish made in Italy in 1535 (plate 20). Although the space has changed its shape—from rectangle to circle—the ornaments filling it have the same static integrity, the same respect for surface and edges, as the ornaments in the embroidery and the carving. This is a matter of style, a sensitivity to modes of organization that the needleworker, carver and potter

12.
Familien Glück (Family Happiness), a pattern for a Berlin-work picture, is engraved on paper and painted with opaque watercolors. As translated from the German, an inscription engraved below the picture reads in part: "Grünthal's art needlework pattern publishing house in Berlin." German, about 1840–60. Height of the picture area: 45.3 cm. (17⅞ in.). Museum of Fine Arts, Boston, gift of Emily Douglas Furness, 1955

13.
This completed Berlin-work version of *Familien Glück* was worked after the pattern illustrated in plate 12. American, about 1840–60. Height as framed (frame not shown): 76.8 cm. (30¼ in.). Museum of Fine Arts, Boston, gift of Emily Douglas Furness, 1958

12

13

14.
During the nineteenth century, needlework patterns like these were collected and kept in albums for reference by women who used them either for their own domestic work or as an aid in earning their livelihood. Shown here are patterns from an album owned by Elizabeth Davish. American, about 1825–50. Cooper-Hewitt Museum, gift of Gertrude Crownfield, 1939

Colorplate 2.
From the embroidery firm of St. Ruf, in France, comes this pattern made by the firm's designers for its needleworkers. The pattern is for a floral design to be worked in the border of a skirt of a formal gown. Gouache on paper. French, about 1780–85. Cooper-Hewitt Museum, gift of the Misses Hewitt, 1920

15

16

15.
Made in Gujarat, India, for export to England, this dyed cotton bed curtain was based on English patterns. 1675–1700. Height: 246 cm. (96¾ in.). Detail. Museum of Fine Arts, Boston, Samuel Putnam Avery Fund and gift of Mrs. Samuel Cabot, 1953

16.
Another Gujarat bed curtain made for export to England, in this case chain-stitched in silk on cotton, shows not only the same pattern but also the same predominantly red and blue-green color scheme. 1675–1700. Height: 260.5 cm. (113½ in.). Detail. Museum of Fine Arts, Boston, Samuel Putnam Avery Fund and gift of Mrs. Samuel Cabot, 1953

17.
In this English needlework version of the same pattern, the bed curtain, of which this is a fragment, was worked with crewels instead of silk. 1675–1725. Height: 66 cm. (26 in.). Museum of Fine Arts, Boston, Elizabeth Day McCormick Collection, 1953

all felt as part of their culture. If they had been using triangles instead of vines, the feeling would have come through just the same. They were all expressing the *style* of Italian art during the Renaissance.

The second example, from a much earlier period, is a fragment of silk needlework from a garment or hanging worked in the eastern Mediterranean region around the seventh century A.D. (plate 21). It exhibits the same stylistic character, as well as the same ornamentation, as the piece of rich silk weaving from the same period and region seen in plate 22. Both textiles show scenes from the New Testament, arranged as though the figures occupy a very shallow space. In the drawing of the figures and in other ways as well, both textile patterns reflect the monumental, static pictorial style of early Byzantine wall mosaics. As in some mosaics, their compositions are contained within circular wreathlike frames. This was particularly well suited to the purposes of textile design, especially in a period when the surface of the composition—whether of plaster, stone or silk—was so important. Our comparison of these two textiles also reveals that needleworkers imitated the appearance of woven silks. Silks were extremely expensive to make since it required complex looms, highly skilled weavers and an enormous outlay of capital to set up a weaving establishment. As we have noted, a needleworker needed very little equip-

19

18

20

18.

Plates 18, 19 and 20 exemplify style in three different decorative arts during the Renaissance. An example of the needlework of the period is the embroidered band in plate 18, which was part of an orphrey or the border of a furnishing fabric. The satin-weave silk foundation was worked with couched silver and gilt cords. Italian or Spanish, 1525–50. Height: 122 cm. (48 in.). Cooper-Hewitt Museum, gift of Bertha Hernstadt, 1961

19.

The arabesque ornament in this detail of a carved walnut choir-stall panel recalls models from both ancient Rome and Renaissance Italy. Italian, 1525–50. Metropolitan Museum of Art, New York, Rogers Fund, 1907

20.

On the border of this round majolica dish—tin-enameled earthenware painted with enamel colors—from the Casa Pirota manufactory in Faenza, Italy, the date has been incorporated into the repeat pattern four times. Italian, 1535. Metropolitan Museum of Art, New York, gift of Julia A. Berwind, 1953

21.

An Egyptian burying ground yielded up this ancient needleworked roundel whose Annunciation scene once adorned a garment or hanging. Eastern Mediterranean, possibly seventh century A.D. Diameter: 17.5 cm. (6⅞ in.). Victoria and Albert Museum, London

22.

This rare piece of silk weaving uses representations of the Annunciation and the Adoration linked by intertwined border garlands as its major motifs. Eastern Mediterranean, possibly seventh century A.D. Diameter of circles: 32 cm. (12⅝ in.). Museo Cristiano, Vatican City

21

22

23

24

23.
In this elegant embroidered dress fabric of silk, architecture and landscape blend in a harmonious fantasy. French, about 1730–40. Height: 100 cm. (39⅜ in.). Detail. Cooper-Hewitt Museum, purchase in memory of Mary Hearn Greims, 1950

24.
Like the embroidered dress fabric in plate 23, this woven one, a brocaded silk, is richly patterned with plants, flowers and graceful buildings, and follows the fashion of arranging pattern elements in isolated "islands." French, about 1730–40. Height: 54 cm. (21¼ in.). Cooper-Hewitt Museum, gift of Lois Clarke, 1952

ment and only a comfortable spot in which to work, and since needleworkers were not limited by the restrictions of a loom they were free to render any pattern they chose at any time. So weavers established the appearance that fine textiles would have, and needleworkers followed suit.

More than a thousand years later needleworkers were still taking their cues from weavers, at least in the matter of luxury fabrics. Any number of examples might have been chosen to illustrate this point. But the one shown here—as our third example of a period style—illustrates this point, and more (plate 23). For it also demonstrates not only the general style of the baroque period in the Europe of the seventeenth and eighteenth centuries but also a particular fashion within that style, a fashion that enjoyed great popularity around 1730–40. The embroidered silk dress fabric in plate 23 shows the fanciful "island" arrangement of natural and manmade elements that characterizes this fashion, that is, the components float in isolation with no bridge or common vantage point linking one unit with another. The woven silk in plate 24 shows the same kinds of ornaments and follows the same "island" arrangement. The arrangement of these ornaments is totally different from the arrangement of the leafy vines in the Renaissance textile, carving and dish. These eighteenth-century flowers, trees and buildings move easily and loosely across the surface they decorate, and the sudden shifts of scale and depth negate the presence of a surface that the Renaissance pieces so clearly respected. We have here, then, an example of a fashion within a style.

Fashions are easier to date than styles because they begin and end more clearly and last for a shorter length of time, and a knowledge of the dates of fashions in any culture helps to determine when a given work of art was produced by that culture. This applies to fashions in ornament as well as to fashions in house furnishings and—particularly—to fashions in clothing. For example, while both the men's waistcoats illustrated here exhibit baroque styles of ornamentation, one of the garments (plate 25) reflects the fashion of the years around 1725–50, when waistcoats were cut with skirts at the sides in front and no collar, and the other is in the fashion of about 1780–90, with its higher waistline, small standing collar and absence of skirts (plate 26). Since the shapes of bed and window hangings, table covers and other furnishing fabrics also changed with fashion, shape is often a major aid to collectors in dating them.

25.
Colorful silk birds and flowers enliven the chevron-quilted linen foundation of this gentleman's waistcoat. English, 1725–50. Museum of Fine Arts, Boston, gift of Mrs. Daryl Parshall, 1961

26.
Amusing chinoiserie motifs, used with elegant restraint, ornament this gentleman's silk waistcoat. The faces of the figures are painted; everything else is embroidered. French, 1780–90. Cooper-Hewitt Museum, bequest of Richard C. Greenleaf, in memory of his mother, Adeline Emma Greenleaf, 1962

25

26

2 Techniques of Needlework

Although this is a book about needlework, and this chapter is about its techniques, it is essential to deal now with needle-work's sister (and often competing) art, weaving, in order to clarify the differences that exist between the two arts. The collector of needlework must develop the ability to distinguish between embroidered and woven fabrics because certain weavings look at first glance very much like embroideries. Some forms of needlework are worked on paper, parchment, bark and leather, among other non-woven foundations, and in those cases it is clear that a needle carrying a yarn made the pattern. But most needlework utilizes a foundation, or ground, of woven fabric, ranging in texture from fine to coarse, and it is not always easy to tell whether the patterns of a finished piece were woven into the fabric or embroidered.

Except in the few cases where very special techniques, such as tablet weaving, which relies on hand-held tablets or cards, are used, textiles are woven on looms. Although the looms may be of varying degrees of complexity, they all have in common certain mechanical devices that enable the weaver to set up a *warp*—a series of yarns running parallel to each other that will run the length of the finished fabric, parallel to its side edges, or *selvedges*. Another device enables the weaver to lift some of the warp yarns on the loom in variable sequences so that a shuttle or bobbin carrying another yarn can be run at a right angle across the warp yarns, from selvedge to selvedge, and deposit a length of this secondary yarn, or *weft*, in the space between the warp yarns that have been lifted and those that remain in their original position. When the raised warp yarns are released, they fall back into their original position and lock the weft yarn into place. Then the weaver lifts a different set of warp yarns and introduces another row, or *shot*, of weft yarn.

The weaving proceeds in this way, row after row, until the warp yarns have been engaged entirely, and warp and wefts have been

Colorplate 3.
Probably worked by a girl trained in a convent, this picture of St. John the Evangelist writing the Apocalypse is one of the embroidered parchment pages in a book of devotional scenes. The parchment is worked with colored silks that show the same pattern on the reverse. The inscriptions are in ink. Probably Spanish, about 1655–65. Height of binding: 14.6 cm. (5¾ in.). Museum of Fine Arts, Boston, Elizabeth Day McCormick Collection, 1943

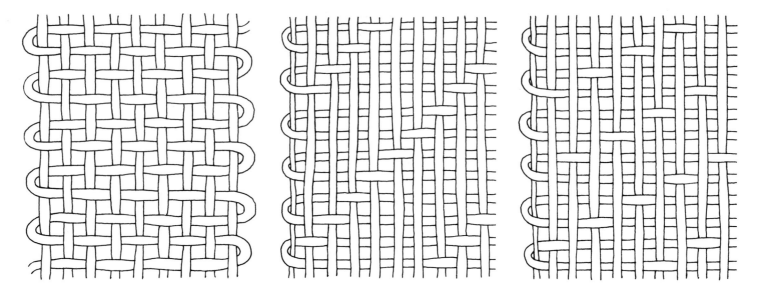

27.
Diagrams of three basic textile weaves. Left to right: plain (tabby) weave, twill weave, satin weave.

interwoven to form a *web*—the finished fabric. By lifting the warp yarns in certain sequences the weaver can produce webs with three basic structures or elaborations of them: *plain weave* (also called *tabby*), in which each weft yarn passes over and under one warp yarn at a time in a regular sequence, producing a basket-weave effect; *twill weave*, in which each weft yarn passes over or under one or more warp yarns in a regular but unequal sequence, producing a diagonal effect; and *satin weave*, in which each weft yarn passes over or under one or more warp yarns in a regular but unequal sequence that is alternated in each row, producing a broken diagonal effect that seems to have no direction at all when viewed from a distance (plate 27).

Despite the diagonal effect that twill and satin weaves give the surface of a fabric, the warp and wefts intersect at right angles as they do in plain weave. In fact, with few exceptions, any extra warp or weft yarns that the weaver introduces to produce a secondary pattern ultimately rest in a right-angle relationship to each other and to the main warp and wefts that form the structure of the web. Such supplementary warp and weft yarns never penetrate each other or the main warp and wefts but lie neatly side by side, however close or encroaching the texture and relative sizes of the yarns may make them seem to be. One may therefore assume that any patterning yarns that lie at an angle other than a right angle to either the warp or weft are embroidery yarns that were introduced into the fabric after it had been taken from the loom—unless further investigation proves that they were placed there by a freely moving shuttle or bobbin during the weaving process. In addition, a pattern yarn that splits a warp or weft yarn or clearly penetrates the fabric through a hole much larger than the normal interstices of the web may be regarded as having been introduced by means of needlework until proved otherwise.

Although these guidelines should enable an observant collector to distinguish readily between needlework and weaving, they cannot take the place of experience and practice. Nevertheless, some works are simple even for the beginner to recognize. Works on nonwoven foundations, for instance, could not be mistaken for anything but needlework. Even works on smooth-surfaced woven fabrics (satins, napped fabrics, fine weaves) are easy to identify as needlework, partly because the directions of the ornamental yarns bear no relation to the warp/weft structure of the foundation and partly because it is readily apparent that the yarns were not laid in the fabric by a bobbin during the weaving process but were pulled through holes made by a needle, sometimes splitting a warp or weft yarn.

Some fabrics, however, may baffle even experts until a detailed technical examination of the piece is made. For example, some kinds of needlework, especially counted-thread work and darning, show pattern yarns that lie neatly parallel to the warp or weft and pass through the normal interstices of the web, never splitting a warp or weft yarn. At first glance this seems to indicate that the pattern yarn was introduced by means of a bobbin or shuttle as the web was being constructed—as, for instance, in overshot or inlaid weaving, in which supplementary weft yarns are woven into the warp. In fact, such pattern yarns could have been introduced with the aid of a needle

28.
Embroidered on an eighteenth-century New England bed curtain, this crewel rose is a characteristic example of the kind of needlework in which the backs of the stitches (left) are obviously a continuation of the pattern yarns on the front (right). American, 1740–60. Detail. Museum of Fine Arts, Boston, gift of Mrs. Jason Westerfield, 1959

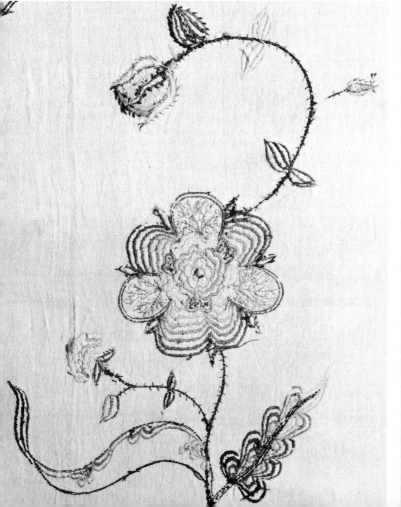

29.
The floral patterns shown here in two views are woven rather than embroidered. The back view of the brocaded leaves at left, showing long, loose, floating yarns that are clearly not the back of stitches, makes this clear even though the short lengths of yarn on the front of the similarly constructed motif at right look superficially like stitches. Pattern details taken from two English brocaded silk dress fabrics, both about 1750–60. Museum of Fine Arts, Boston, respectively Elizabeth Day McCormick Collection, 1943, and gift of Amelia Peabody and William S. Eaton, 1946

after the foundation fabric was removed from the loom. To distinguish needlework from patterned weaving in cases like this requires a good deal of knowledge and experience, and the ground rules offered above provide only the most elementary guide to acquiring it.

The backs of patterned fabrics offer more clues to the method of construction than the fronts do, but here again there is no simple, single, absolute way of distinguishing woven patterns from embroidered ones. In the case of very rich patterns, it is easier to determine which method was used. For instance, the elaborate flower in plate 28 was embroidered after its foundation fabric was removed from the loom. On the front (right) are stitches set in random directions, and on the back (left) are segments of the same yarns, whose size, direction and tension clearly show that they are continuations of the stitches that appear on the front. In another fabric of the same period and style (plate 29, right), pattern yarns lie neatly in rows on the front, each segment of yarn superficially resembling a darning stitch. The back of this kind of construction, illustrated in a different but similar fabric (plate 29, left), tells quite a different story: here the pattern yarns puff out and run free for great distances above the surface of the web, showing that they are not the backs of stitches but lengths of *brocading* yarn running on the back where the pattern does not require them on the front of the fabric. The pattern is clearly a woven one. Brocaded (and the closely related inlaid) fabrics present a special problem because the pattern yarns are in a sense "embroidered" on the warp, in the weft direction, as the web is being constructed; the weaver "embroiders" the pattern on the warp by weaving through it bobbins carrying supplementary wefts of different colors. The bobbin carrying any one of these supplementary colors may be excluded from one or more rows of weaving and left hanging at the back of the web while the foundation weave continues to grow. When the idle bobbin is picked up again as required by the pattern, its yarn may leave a diagonal trace on the back of the fabric and might therefore be mistaken for an embroidery yarn. However, no brocading (or inlaid) yarn ever penetrates a warp or weft yarn.

Throughout the long and complex history of textiles, countless special techniques have created all sorts of fabrics that can puzzle even experts. Such mavericks occur frequently among fabrics from so-called primitive cultures like that of pre-Conquest Peru, which has given us some of the most sophisticated manipulations of yarn imaginable, and also from folk cultures where the needleworkers frequently seem to have been imitating costly woven fabrics. But we also have textiles of ambiguous character from societies with advanced technologies, like those of Europe and America in the eighteenth and nineteenth centuries. They have left us with such oddities as woven imitations of white quilts (*marseilles quilting*) and cross sections of compressed packets of yarn glued to canvas that look for all the world like fine patterned velvets or rugs or pile embroidery (*Crossley mosaics*). These examples are offered only to alert the reader to the fact that it is not always easy to identify needlework for what it is. Each new problem must be studied on its own terms. Human ingenuity is too great, and human imagination too fertile, to allow for easy definitions and consistent performance in the manifold expressions of needlework and weaving.

Considering needlework now apart from its relation to weaving, we could say in broad terms that anything made with a needle can be called needlework. But the purpose of this book is to introduce the reader to a kind of textile art specifically defined as one in which a foundation structure or membrane (woven or nonwoven) has been ornamented with yarns or objects applied with a needle. Such a definition immediately eliminates tailoring and simple seaming. More-over, needlework so defined is not synonymous with embroidery, for embroidery can include applications to a surface through the use of glue, staples, studs or any other adhesive material as well as by means of needle stitches. Nor does the term needlework as used in this book include fabrics created through the interaction of yarn and a needle or hook, such as knitted, netted or crocheted fabrics or any other so-called single-element fabrics, or knotted fabrics such as macramé. Finally, needlework as used here refers specifically to handwork and not to machine embroidery.

Needlepoint laces constitute a gray area in this classification. Some were needle*worked* on a base of another fabric; others were needle-

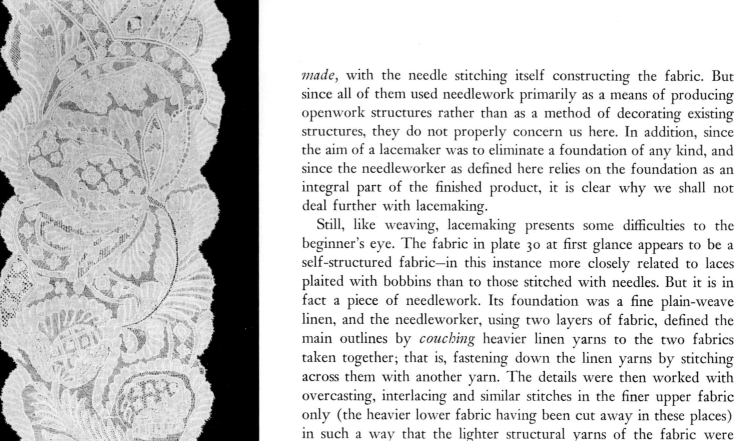

30

made, with the needle stitching itself constructing the fabric. But since all of them used needlework primarily as a means of producing openwork structures rather than as a method of decorating existing structures, they do not properly concern us here. In addition, since the aim of a lacemaker was to eliminate a foundation of any kind, and since the needleworker as defined here relies on the foundation as an integral part of the finished product, it is clear why we shall not deal further with lacemaking.

Still, like weaving, lacemaking presents some difficulties to the beginner's eye. The fabric in plate 30 at first glance appears to be a self-structured fabric—in this instance more closely related to laces plaited with bobbins than to those stitched with needles. But it is in fact a piece of needlework. Its foundation was a fine plain-weave linen, and the needleworker, using two layers of fabric, defined the main outlines by *couching* heavier linen yarns to the two fabrics taken together; that is, fastening down the linen yarns by stitching across them with another yarn. The details were then worked with overcasting, interlacing and similar stitches in the finer upper fabric only (the heavier lower fabric having been cut away in these places) in such a way that the lighter structural yarns of the fabric were pulled slightly out of their normal positions, thereby creating tiny open

31

30.
Deflected-element embroidery was used to create this lacelike lappet, or pendant, from a cap for a lady of fashion. Northern European, perhaps Danish, 1700–1750. Length: 51.5 cm. (20¼ in.). Detail. Cooper-Hewitt Museum, bequest of Richard C. Greenleaf, in memory of his mother, Adeline Emma Greenleaf, 1962

31.
The pattern drawn on the linen foundation to guide the needleworker is clearly seen in this partly worked picture of the Sacrifice of Isaac. English, 1650–1700. Height: 58 cm. (22¾ in.). Cooper-Hewitt Museum, gift of Irwin Untermyer, 1959

spaces that add to the decorative effect of the stitches. Since the structural elements (the warp and weft yarns) of the base fabric were deflected from their normal paths, this kind of work is referred to as *deflected-element embroidery*.

Needleworkers throughout the centuries have depended on the structure of the foundation membrane to achieve other decorative effects as well. *Canvas work* and *counted-thread work* are both based on this principle. Canvas work is best known today in the form of needlepoint, a procedure in which the needleworker uses a woven foundation with a rather open texture and a markedly square weave. This woven foundation is called the canvas. The worker uses the grid or mesh of the canvas as a guide in placing the stitches. In the past, as now, the foundation fabrics for some canvas work have patterns drawn or painted on them (plate 31). If the pattern has curved lines cutting across the grid of the weave, the needleworker has to decide which holes in the mesh should take the needle in order to give the illusion that the line is continuous and not—as technically it has to be—a line broken into tiny steps. The smaller the mesh, the smaller the stitches can be, and the more convincing the curve. Small, slanted, single stitches (tent stitches) like those in plate 31 came to be known as *petit point*, larger ones as *gros point*. Sometimes a needleworker used both in a single work in order to achieve some special effect.

Other kinds of canvas work, and many classes of needlework that show foundation weaves with less pronounced grids, were patterned by counting threads in the foundation and placing each stitch at the warp/weft coordinates designated by the position of a symbol representing that stitch on a separate pattern sheet (plate 12, see page 17). Counted-thread work like this required a great deal of attention and patience, but it cost the needleworker less to make than work that required the pattern to be drawn or painted on the foundation fabric. Especially in provincial societies, where money was scarce and access to painted or published patterns was limited, needleworkers used the counted-thread method on plain-weave cottons or linens. When doing canvas or counted-thread work, needleworkers in the past used a special selection of stitches that lent themselves particularly well to the square-mesh system. These were traditionally tent, cross, Gobelin, darning and running stitches (see page 120), but almost any stitch proper to decorative needlework could be used.

At the other end of the scale, needleworkers, as we have noted, have used such nonwoven foundations as paper, parchment, bark and leather, or such smooth-surfaced fabrics as satin, broadcloth and other napped textiles, or fine-scale plain-weave fabrics that scarcely show the warp/weft system at all. In these cases the needle can move freely, without regard for the structure of the foundation.

In needlework, paper and parchment have been used primarily as a base for embroidered pictures. Such embroideries in Western cultures

32.
Some convent-trained North American Indian girl probably worked this drawstring purse. Combining European and Indian traditions, the front and back panels of birchbark show floral sprays embroidered with colored moose hair in flat and knotted stitches. French Canadian or American, about 1800–1820. Height of bark panels: 14.6 cm. (5¾ in.). Cooper-Hewitt Museum, gift of Mrs. William P. Treadwell, 1916

run the gamut from the delicate silk pictures of flowers or saints meticulously worked by highly skilled girls in convent schools in the seventeenth century to the brash punched cards meant to be laced with bright wool yarns and hung as pictures on the walls of late nineteenth-century rooms. The seventeenth-century embroidered paper or parchment pictures, called *colifichets* in French, were usually worked so that the image was equally well executed front and back and could be displayed between two sheets of glass in a frame or mounted as leaves in an album or book (colorplate 3).

The native peoples of North America traditionally used bark as a foundation to be embroidered with porcupine or bird quills, moose hair or other decorative materials. Ursuline nuns who went to French Canada in the seventeenth century adopted some of these techniques and before long were teaching Indian girls in convents to work their traditional dyed moose hair on birchbark with European patterns and in nontraditional forms that blended the two cultures with surprising success (plate 32).

The types of needlework discussed thus far depend on the application of pattern yarns, usually of many colors, to a woven foundation fabric or other ground. Most needlework of this kind produces textiles that are essentially flat, though the pattern yarns may give the fabric some appearance of relief. Other major categories of needlework depend for their effect on the use of high relief. In many cultures needleworkers applied thick fancy yarns, metal, wood, bone or other nontextile materials to the surface of the foundation in order to produce sculptural effects. This is usually called *raised work*, a term used for any form of needlework that incorporates padded fabrics, spiraled wires or tinsels, beads or other three-dimensional materials made separately and then sewn to the foundation, which itself generally has been prepared with flat stitches to outline or in some other way guide the placement of the applications. *Stump work*, a nineteenth-century term for a type of raised work, refers only to a particular class of needlework that was practiced primarily in England during the seventeenth century but had already been anticipated elsewhere in Europe for use on ecclesiastical vestments in the Middle Ages. It then was revived briefly in the nineteenth century (plates 48 and 104, see pages 57 and 117). In stump work the high-relief effect was achieved both by covering padding materials or bits of sculptured wood with silk fabrics and by working knitted or woven fabrics in relief above the level of the foundation fabric, often leaving one or more edges free of the ground. Examples of raised work that have come down to us from Western European cultures over the centuries include magnificent book or box covers (plate 33), pictures, mirror frames and vestment ornaments.

Quilting is another form of needlework that depends on an element of relief and a play of light and shadow for its effect. The needle-

33.
In this splendid example of a sixteenth-century raised-work box or book cover, metal yarns and brightly colored silks create rich iridescent effects, a silver salamander crouches at the base of a golden tree, and coral beads dot the surrounding areas. Probably French, 1575–1625. Height: 33 cm. (13 in.). Cooper-Hewitt Museum, gift of Marian Hague, 1959

34

34.
Padded and quilted coverlets like this one from New England used wool fabrics for both the front and back for greater warmth. American, 1750–1800. Length: 253 cm. (99¼ in.). Museum of Fine Arts, Boston, gift of Francis H. Bigelow, 1924

35.
No quilting stitches were used to make this applied-work coverlet. The birds and flowers were cut from an English woodblock-printed cotton of about 1780 and applied to the plain-weave linen foundation. The initials PW on the urn are probably those of Phebe Warner, daughter of the maker, Anne Walgrave Warner of New York. American, about 1800–1803. Height: 264 cm. (104 in.). Metropolitan Museum of Art, New York, gift of Catherine E. Cotheal, 1938

worker makes stitches through two layers of fabric, which are not necessarily identical. Sometimes a layer of wadding material lies between the two textiles and puffs up to form tiny mounds between the rows of stitches (plate 34). Alternatively, the needleworker may define the main motifs with pairs of parallel rows of stitches and then run a cord through the resulting narrow slots. The thickness of the cord separates the two layers of fabric in those places, again giving the surface a relief effect.

Quilting was often combined with other forms of needlework in a single piece, and sometimes the other work makes a more dramatic effect than the quilting. This is particularly evident in coverlets whose main pattern depends on pieced or applied work (plates 68–70, see pages 76 and 78). However, not all pieced or applied work was also quilted (plate 35). Needleworkers often used pieced or applied work to create elaborately patterned furnishing fabrics on a grand scale, especially hangings for altars, walls and windows (plates 43 and 86, see pages 48 and 97) and also covers for furniture. By using these techniques instead of working with needle stitches and yarns, a needleworker could cover such large surfaces more quickly, and a patron who ordered pieced or applied work instead of stitchery or elaborately patterned woven fabrics could get custom designs for house and wardrobe more cheaply. The more common form of applied work involves stitching on one layer of plain or patterned fabric above the last; the design elements decrease in size as they rise. In the less frequently used technique of reverse applied work, the design elements decrease in size as they descend (colorplate 28, see page 113).

35

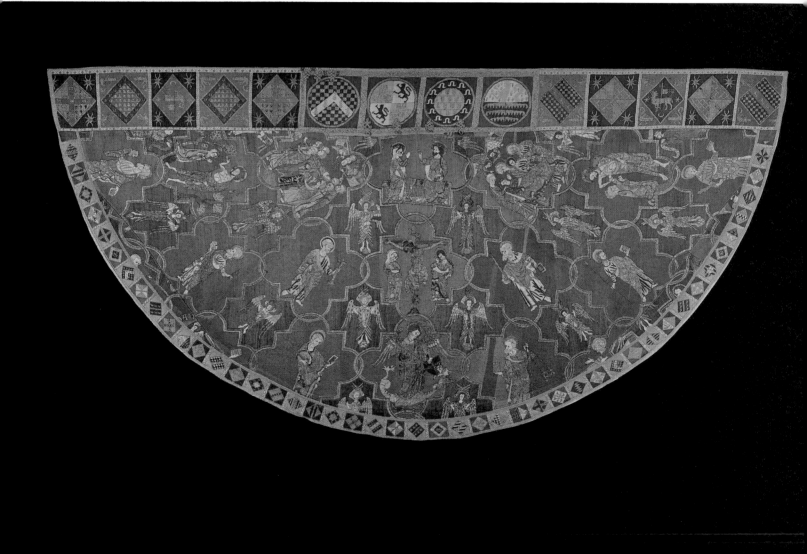

3   Mainstreams in the West

Every technique discussed so far appears in Western needle-work, as we trace it from the beginnings to the present day. Both amateur and professional embroiderers have created a varied body of work, from tiny purses to monumental wall hangings, from a charmingly naive petticoat border to the sublime Syon Cope—that brilliant vestment from the hands of English needleworkers that shone during Mass with all the light of the Christian Church.

Needleworkers in the West produced work for home, church and royal court. The record they left in their work documents the social, political and economic history of the human race as clearly as our paintings and buildings do. But the materials and methods of needlework are very special. They have a sensual quality all their own and appeal to the human mind and emotions in an entirely distinctive way.

Egypt's climate and the burial customs of her ancient people worked hand in hand to preserve what are the oldest embroideries we know of today, now in the Cairo Museum. The earliest and most famous of these are pieces from the tombs of the pharaoh Thutmose IV (c. 1419–1386 B.C.) and the now fabulous boy-king Tutankhamun (1334–1325 B.C.) The earliest embroidery, associated with Thutmose IV, is a fragment of a larger fabric and shows pink and green rosettes worked in satin stitches, all in linen yarns. The pieces from Tutankhamun's tomb are all garments. One of them, a tunic, has needlework bordering the neckline, the sides and the bottom; the pattern features exquisitely drawn flowers, animals and sphinxes. Needleworkers decorated these garments with chain and stem stitches, padded work and motifs of thin metal stitched to the foundation fabric.

Other examples of decorative needlework from remote times in the Western world include a linen fragment with needle holes tracing a pattern of single lions in a lozenge trellis (now in the Victoria and Albert Museum in London), which is Greek and dates from the fifth

Colorplate 4.
Originally made as a chasuble (the medieval form—long all around, with points front and back) but later remodeled as a cope with the orphrey and perimeter band taken from other vestments, this vestment is known as the Syon Cope. It exemplifies the superb quality of the needlework known throughout medieval Europe as *opus anglicanum*. English, about 1300–1320. Victoria and Albert Museum, London, 1864

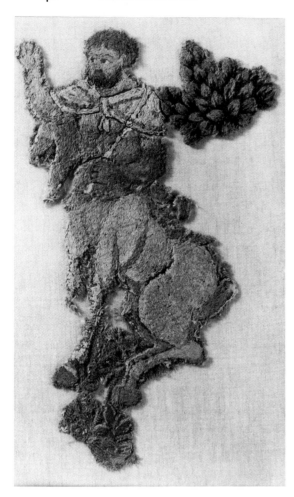

36.
One of the few embroideries to survive from ancient times is this Hellenistic-style fragment with a centaur worked in white linen and colored wool yarns. Eastern Mediterranean, fourth–fifth century A.D. Height: 34 cm. (13⅜ in.). Detail. Musée Historique des Tissus, Lyons

century B.C. Some fragments of needlework with flowers and figures dating from sometime between the fourth and first centuries B.C. were found in the Crimea and are now in the Hermitage in Leningrad. The great majority of textiles found in Egyptian burying grounds of the early Christian Era are tapestry woven, but a few have patterns executed in needlework. A piece in the style of Hellenistic Greece, dating from about the fourth or fifth century A.D., shows a marvelously drawn and worked figure of a centaur (plate 36). A hanging of about the same period has a pattern of trees rendered in a less naturalistic style (plate 37). This is one of several works of the fourth to seventh centuries A.D. that exhibit the growing taste for stylized drawing that blossomed forth under the rulers of Byzantium (see also plate 21, page 23).

Coming closer to our own times, we find that many pieces of English, German, Spanish and western Islamic needlework dating from the eighth to twelfth centuries have survived. The best known and historically most important of these is the extraordinary Bayeux Tapestry, which illustrates incidents in the conquest of England by the Normans under William the Conqueror in 1066. Believed to have been worked in England about 1080 at the order of Bishop Odo of Bayeux, half brother of William the Conqueror, the famous "tapestry," despite its name, is embroidered rather than tapestry woven, and is worked on a plain-weave linen foundation with colored wool yarns. Its renown stems from the fact that, rightly or wrongly, it has been regarded as an eyewitness account of a tremendously important event in British history. It is also probably the largest embroidery in existence, more than 70 meters (nearly 231 feet) long and 50 centimeters (about 19½ inches) wide (plate 38).

While the Bayeux embroidery was made in a secular context, most of the work surviving from the Middle Ages is ecclesiastical because churches took great pains to preserve the vestments and other decorations made for them. And the church played an enormous role in the development of needlework everywhere. Religious ritual demanded special and often elaborate garments for the clergy. Special hangings and covers were made to ornament religious buildings and instruct the congregation. The subject of ecclesiastical needlework is complex and deserves a more detailed study than we can give it here, but it is important to discuss it at least briefly since so many vestments are to be found in museums and on the market.

In the Roman and Protestant churches of Christendom the chief needleworked garments worn by the clergy have been albs, copes, dalmatics, tunicles, chasubles, stoles and maniples. These developed characteristic shapes and ornaments early in the history of the Roman Church. The alb was a white ankle-length garment decorated with lace or embroidery, which was worn under some of the others. The cope originally took the form of a long cloak complete with hood.

In the twelfth century it became a semicircle of sumptuous woven or embroidered fabric with a vestigial hood that eventually became a flat shield resting on the back across the shoulders. The cope had a decorative band, or orphrey, applied along the straight side; this was usually ornamented with needlework, sometimes depicting subjects taken from the New Testament or the lives of the saints. (One can glean a notion of the resplendence of the gilt yarns used in early orphreys from the fact that the name comes from the Latin *auriphrygium*, meaning Phrygian gold, referring to the ancient Phrygians of Asia Minor, who were renowned for their gold embroideries.) The cope's hood was also ornamented with needlework. The dalmatic and the very similar tunicle were tunics made of equally splendid woven or embroidered material and had orphreys (here also called apparels) in the form of strips as well as others shaped like rectangles or trapezoids; these had either ornamental motifs or pictures with Christian subjects. Chasubles were originally cone shaped and fell to the floor all around the body like a bell (hence the term *bell chasuble*). By the end of the fifteenth century the vestment had taken the shape of two shields joined at the shoulders. The back panel was rectangular with curved bottom edges, and the front panel was cut away near the top to allow the arms to move forward freely; the resultant shape, with sloping shoulders, indented upper sides and curved bottom edges, resembles the body of a violin (plate 39). Chasubles have orphreys on the front and back. The stole and maniple represent the earlier liturgical scarf and handkerchief; the first took the shape of a long strip of woven or embroidered fabric with trapezoidal ends; the maniple was similar but much shorter. They were ornamented with floral designs and crosses.

During the early Middle Ages Spain encompassed the cultures of both Christianity and Islam. Among the handsome and sumptuous vestments that have survived from twelfth-century Spain is the chasuble of St. Thomas Becket, which was worked in gilt yarns on silk in Almería. This important example, now in the Cathedral of Fermo in Italy, shows the style of Islamic art of that period, in the hands of superb Muslim embroiderers. Another example of Islamic work for the Christian Church is the coronation mantle of the Holy Roman emperors made in Palermo, Sicily, in 1133–34, with gilt yarns, pearls and enamels on silk (now in the Schatzkammer in Vienna).

Christian needleworkers who were active in Spain at that time have also left us a number of impressive monuments, chief of which is the great Creation banner or hanging in the Cathedral of Gerona. It is clearly dependent on the Romanesque style of painting, and we can date it in the twelfth century. The great set of embroidered altar furnishings made for the bishop of Osma, Spain, about 1468 is one of the most important examples of later Spanish Christian work to have survived; it is now in the Art Institute of Chicago.

37.
Leafy trees are arranged in schematic fashion on this linen hanging found in an Egyptian grave. Eastern Mediterranean, fourth–fifth century A.D. Height: 157.5 cm. (62 in.); trees: 17–25 cm. (6¾–10 in.). Detail. Victoria and Albert Museum, London

VLV · TENENS · CONFOR... ... hIC EST: ... DVX

VVILT

38.
In this section of the Bayeux Tapestry, which illustrates the story of the Norman conquest of England in 1066, William the Conqueror, raising his visor, turns to spur on his men. English, about 1080. Height: 49.5 cm. (19½ in.). Museum of the Cathedral of Bayeux, France

Colorplate 5.
Believed to have been worked by fourteenth-century nuns, this church hanging depicts Aaron's Rod and Gideon's Fleece, among other biblical subjects. Heraldic devices and figures of saints decorate the borders. Faces and inscriptions are painted on the linen foundation; other elements are stitched with colored silks. German, about 1375–1400. Height: 160 cm. (63 in.). Detail. Metropolitan Museum of Art, New York, gift of Mrs. W. Murray Crane, 1969

At the height of the Middle Ages nuns and probably also secular professional needleworkers in Germany produced enormous quantities of vestments and hangings. A portion of a large hanging worked in Lower Saxony late in the fourteenth century (colorplate 5) combines needlework, done in colored silks, and painting, done directly on the fabric, for the faces and inscriptions. The complete hanging would have been too large for an altar; it may have hung in a church over a row of choir stalls, as tapestries of this size often did. The main composition shows incidents from the life of Christ and Old Testament scenes presented as prefigurations. Figures of saints and coats of arms fill the upper and lower borders.

During the thirteenth and fourteenth centuries English needlework, referred to in church inventories in Latin as *opus anglicanum* (English work), was the most highly prized of any in the West, and was sought by churches in many parts of Europe for the supreme quality of its design and workmanship. Most of the surviving examples are ecclesiastical vestments. Among the best preserved and richest of these is the great cope from the Brigittine convent at Syon in Middlesex (colorplate 4). Most of it was worked in underside couching with colored silks and gilt and silver yarns; the flesh and drapery were worked with colored silks in delicate split stitches. The design represents scenes from the lives of Christ and the Virgin and includes figures of the Apostles. The orphrey running along the straight edge and the narrow band stitched along the curve display heraldic shields, a kind of pattern used fairly often at this period. Since medieval

39

40

39.
Baroque motifs worked in couched and laid gilt yarns and tapes decorate this sumptuous silk velvet chasuble. Southern European, 1700–1750. Museum of Fine Arts, Boston, gift of Philip Lehman "in memory of my wife, Carrie L. Lehman," 1938

40.
This epigonation—a stiffened liturgical kerchief worn by Eastern Orthodox priests—is completely covered with couched gilt and silver yarns. The figures are outlined with red silk yarns, and the flesh portions are worked with colored silks. Eastern European, perhaps Greek or Russian, seventeenth century or later. Length: 36.8 cm. (14½ in.). Cooper-Hewitt Museum, gift of Mrs. Rudolf M. Riefstahl, 1957

needleworkers did not customarily sign their work, we do not know who designed or embroidered these great English vestments. Some were probably made by nuns, others certainly by professional embroiderers, some perhaps by monks.

Professional embroiderers working for the church in England did not neglect secular embroideries. In addition to their labors for the church, they made splendid things for secular use—clothing, horse trappings (the fabrics made to cover the chests and backs of horses in parades), banners, palls, hangings and so on—though very few of these works have survived. Some handsome pieces in the Cluny Museum in Paris show the heraldic leopards of England, together with foliage and human figures. Worked around 1330–40 with gilt and colored silk yarns, embellished with pearls and bits of crystal backed with gold foil, these pieces may originally have formed part of horse trappings; they were later used for ecclesiastical vestments.

Other important medieval vestments, like the so-called dalmatic of Charlemagne dating from the fourteenth century, which is in the Treasury of St. Peter's Basilica in the Vatican, show the highly stylized drawing characteristic of late Byzantine art. This style continued to be used as the model for needlework on Eastern Orthodox Church vestments for centuries (plates 40 and 41).

We have already met, in the discussion of professional embroiderers, with Jacopo Campi and Geri Lapi, two of the brilliant Italian professionals who brought international fame to Florentine needlework during the fourteenth and fifteenth centuries. Toward the end of that period Flemish embroiderers achieved a standard of excellence that had not been seen since the golden days of *opus anglicanum*, a hundred years earlier. One of the greatest achievements of the professional Flemish needleworkers has survived and is now in the Schatzkammer in Vienna. It is the set of vestments for the Mass made about 1425–75 for the Order of the Golden Fleece, probably in Brussels. It comprises three copes, a tunicle, a dalmatic, and hangings to be placed above and in front of an altar.

As the Renaissance flowered in Italy during the fifteenth and sixteenth centuries, Italian painters found new ways to represent real space and distance, and their discoveries naturally passed into the hands of needleworkers. What followed was a new class of needlework—embroidered pictures that, but for the materials used, were Renaissance paintings. Countless embroidered pictures must have been made in direct imitation of wall or easel paintings at this period, and some of them have survived. With few exceptions they were made as decorations for ecclesiastical vestments and hangings, above all as

41.
Worked with colored silks and gilt and silver yarns, and bearing an inscription identifying the maker as "the nun Anastasia," this silk epitaphios sindon (a shroud for the ceremonial bier of Christ used on Good Friday in Eastern Orthodox churches) comes from the region of Georgia in the Caucasus. Seventeenth–eighteenth century. Length: 191.8 cm. (75½ in.). Detroit Institute of Arts, gift of Mr. and Mrs. James O. Keene, 1953

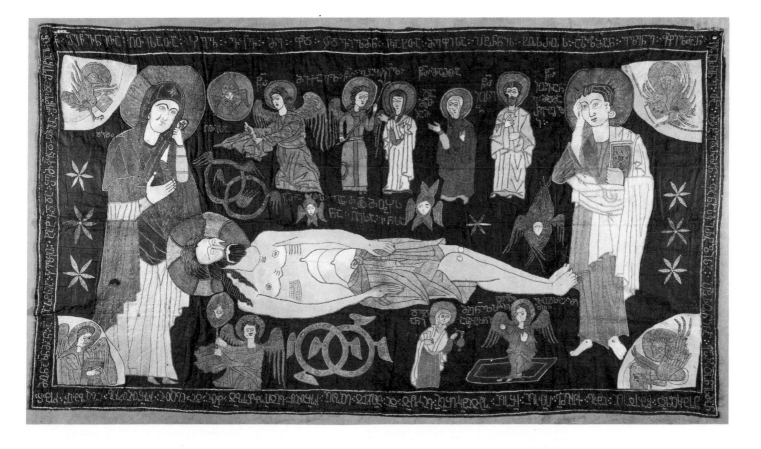

orphreys on dalmatics, hoods of copes and sections of altar frontals or dossals. One of these pictures, attributed to a Ferrara needleworker about 1475–1500, depicts the Birth of the Virgin (plate 42). It is worked with colored silk and gilt yarns in a variety of stitches and an elegant technique called in French *or nué* (shaded gold), which gives parts of the composition the appearance of translucent enamel. To achieve this effect, needleworkers stitched over couched gilt yarns with finer, more widely spaced colored silks. The glint of the gold shines through between the silk stitches and gives the finished work an extraordinary luminosity. Throughout ensuing centuries, both professional and amateur needleworkers in the West continued to embroider pictures, some to be framed and others of much larger size to be hung as tapestries, for churches, homes and public buildings.

Along with pictorial work, ornamental embroidery flourished in Europe. During the fifteenth and sixteenth centuries, large quantities of applied work were produced, and a great many pieces have survived. Plain silk, velvets and patterned weavings were cut up and made into bed and window hangings, banners, ceremonial robes, wall hangings, cushion and furniture covers and countless other articles for home and church (plate 43). Other pieces, however, called for regular stitchery, with smaller forms worked in finer materials, and some of the most sumptuous silk and metal embroideries that have come down to us date from the sixteenth century. One of the most impressive pieces is a Spanish table carpet worked with silk and silver yarns on linen canvas (colorplate 6), which gives an effect midway between that of a fine silk carpet and the sleek coat of a cat.

Embroideries as elaborate in design and execution as this were certainly the work of professionals. But we also have countless examples of amateur needlework from the sixteenth and seventeenth centuries. The largest group of these embroideries includes the borders of sheets, towels, cushion covers and other household linens, and also garments, worked with silk on linen foundations. The work was usually executed with one shade of silk, most often red or green, occasionally yellow, blue, violet or brown; less frequently two shades were used. Cross, running and back stitches are most common (plate 44 and see also plate 6, page 14). The patterns, taken from sixteenth- and seventeenth-century books that were published for this purpose (plate 7, see page 14), offered everything from biblical, mythological and fanciful figures to leafy vines and branches. In some cases the background was solidly covered with stitches, leaving the white of the linen ground to carry the figured area of the pattern. This kind of work survived in the Mediterranean region—particularly in parts of Italy, the Greek islands and Morocco—into the twentieth century (plate 105, see page 117). It is important to remember this fact when attempting to date a Mediterranean embroidery of this sort.

42.
The conventions for representing reality that were developed in the art of painting in Renaissance Italy clearly influenced the design of this embroidered depiction of the Birth of the Virgin. Italian, 1475–1500. Height: 32.5 cm. (12¾ in.). Metropolitan Museum of Art, New York, gift of Irwin Untermyer, 1964

In the seventeenth and eighteenth centuries pictorial embroidery in the baroque style blossomed. Great hangings were made for domestic interiors; they were worked either in tent, cross or other canvas stitches or in long and short, split, satin and other stitches that enabled the needleworker to approximate the smooth effect of painting. One of the finest and most famous needle paintings of the period, now in the Victoria and Albert Museum, is an Adoration of the Shepherds signed and dated on the back: "Edmund Harrison Imbroderer to King Charles made theis Anno Dom. 1637." It is a small picture, only 109.2 centimeters (43 inches) high, but it is technically and artistically like numbers of wall-size needle paintings that have come down to us from France, Italy and Spain. During the seventeenth century girls trained as needleworkers at the St. Joseph de la Providence home for girls in Paris made large wall hangings as well as magnificent furniture covers. The examples we know are worked in tent stitch with colored wool and silk yarns combined with gilt yarns couched in fancy patterns. Gabriel de Saint-Aubin, who published a treatise on the art of the embroiderer in 1770, said rather disparagingly of tent stitch that it was "easy work," and added that needleworkers in religious communities used it a good deal. It is hard to share his unflattering opinion of this work when we look at the set of four wall hangings probably made at St. Joseph de la Providence about 1683 and now in the Metropolitan Museum of Art. The hanging

43.
Applied work in satin fabric and gilt cords created the arcades that decorate this velvet hanging. Probably Spanish, 1550–1600. Height: 57.8 cm. (22¾ in.). Metropolitan Museum of Art, New York, Rogers Fund, 1906

44.
This kind of border for a household furnishing fabric was usually worked at home by girls or women following one of the many printed pattern books published for their use. Italian, 1550–1625. Height: 12.8 cm. (5 in.). Metropolitan Museum of Art, New York, gift of Marian Hague, 1916

illustrated here (see frontispiece), which is 274.5 centimeters wide and more than 411 centimeters tall (9 feet by more than 13½ feet), represents Spring. The other three panels represent Summer, Air and Fire; it is believed that they once were accompanied by four other hangings showing the remaining seasons and elements.

During this period, which saw the full flowering of baroque painting in Europe, every kind of textile object—whether a garment or a furnishing—was regarded as suitable for embroidered decoration, even a tiny purse no more than a few centimeters high (colorplate 7). Toward the end of the eighteenth century French needleworkers produced an impressive number of large silk panels worked in chain stitch. These were probably made with the help of a hook and a tambour frame rather than a needle, in order to save time. Many of these embroideries resemble fine brocaded silks of the same period, specifically the ones in the style of the great silk designer Philippe de Lasalle (plate 45).

Within this one group of woven and embroidered silks we can trace the development of the late baroque style into the so-called neoclassical style at the end of the eighteenth century. It was more than just a change in fashion; it was in fact the emergence of a new mentality in European culture, one concerned with the deliberate and romantic revival of styles of the past. This is the mentality that motivated designers around 1800 to develop what we now call, too simply, the Empire style. The mentality behind that "style" contained seeds that were to blossom for the next hundred years, as the nineteenth century pursued its passion for exotica and the revival of ancient, medieval, Renaissance and baroque forms and ornaments.

Many factors brought this change about, but there can be no doubt that both cultural and political developments during the second half of the eighteenth century fostered a taste for motifs and compositions derived from ancient Greece, Rome and Egypt. Systematic archaeological excavations were undertaken at Herculaneum and Pompeii during the middle and second half of the century and the findings were published; France, no longer a monarchy, and the new nation forming in North America both looked to ancient Greece and Rome for their ideals of a republic; and the end of the century saw the rise of Napoleon Bonaparte, who thought of himself as a Roman emperor and who extended the power of France into Egypt. Fashionable women dressed in what they regarded as ancient styles, and the wealthier among them furnished their houses with textiles bearing the motifs of antiquity. A number of these splendid embroideries have survived. One of them (plate 46) was worked after patterns in the style of another great French silk designer of the period, Jean-François Bony, with applied silks and colored silk and silver yarns in chain stitch.

Colorplate 6.
In the past, the decoration of any elegant
room usually included rich textiles like
this sumptuous embroidered silk and
silver table carpet. Worked in Spain, the
covering is a splendid example of luxury
needlework. Sixteenth century. Length:
239 cm. (94 in.). Museum of Fine Arts,
Boston, Harriet Otis Cruft Fund, 1956

Colorplate 7.
On each side of this diminutive purse a
figure only a few centimeters high has
been worked with incredible clarity—a
shepherd on one side, a shepherdess on
the other. German, about 1740–60.
Height: 11 cm. (4¼ in.). Cooper-Hewitt
Museum, bequest of Richard C. Greenleaf, in memory of his mother, Adeline
Emma Greenleaf, 1962

45.
Woven silks in the style of the celebrated Philippe de Lasalle influenced the pattern of this satin wall panel worked with colored silk yarns. French, about 1775–90. Height: 323 cm. (127 in.). Metropolitan Museum of Art, New York, gift of the Samuel H. Kress Foundation, 1958

46.
In this neoclassical wall panel showing the urns and other motifs revived from antiquity that were so popular at the end of the eighteenth century, the chain-stitched parts were probably worked with a hook rather than a needle to save time. French, after a design by Jean-François Bony, about 1800–1805. Height: 254 cm. (100 in.). Metropolitan Museum of Art, New York, Rogers Fund, 1923

The story of needlework in the West from this moment onward becomes truly international, and it is not feasible in this book to trace individual developments in the leading nations of Europe and America. However, since the domestic needlework of both Great Britain and the United States in the nineteenth century developed especially interesting forms—great quantities of which survive—it will be worthwhile to look at that period from the point of view of these two cultures. A brief backward glance, beginning with the English tradition, the older of the two, will help us to see how each civilization developed its own traditions of needlework in the preceding centuries.

The great tradition of professional needlework, the so-called *opus anglicanum*, that won international fame for English embroiderers in the Middle Ages seems to have disappeared about 1500. Although no domestic embroideries have survived from that period, we have masses of expertly worked costume and furnishing fabrics from sixteenth- and seventeenth-century England. Therefore, we have to assume that the domestic embroiderers of those centuries were working in an earlier domestic tradition that set the standards and developed their extraordinary skill with the needle.

The other extraordinary thing about this group of domestic embroideries is their uniqueness, the fact that they are so totally British, so unlike work of the same period on the continent of Europe—except for the canvas-work furnishing fabrics, which maintained an international look. But the patterns on coifs, bodices, waistcoats, jackets, purses, gloves, caps, stomachers, book covers, cushion and pillow covers, and bed hangings constitute a particular national language based on a celebration of the English garden with its roses, carnations, daffodils, honeysuckle, columbines and irises, and also on the British love for birds, beasts and insects (plate 9 and colorplate 11, see pages 15 and 72). These are not the motifs found in German and Italian pattern books of the period. They were instead developed from illustrations in books on plants and beasts, and from the same sources that Thomas Trevelyon used in compiling his design manuscripts of 1608 and 1616 (plate 8, see page 15). Professional embroiderers were active in England at this time, and we may assume that they made up, sold or otherwise circulated these patterns and that they sometimes drew out the patterns on foundation fabrics for women to work at home. Perhaps when a project was too ambitious for the lady of the house, a professional embroiderer's services might be sought out. The richly patterned table carpet in plate 47 might have been made in such circumstances.

English work dating from about 1550 to 1700 is cohesive not only in its artistic character but in its technical aspects. Embroiderers used silk and metal yarns and fancy purls and tinsels (decorative metallic materials used as yarns) in a variety of stitches, most characteristically raised stitches, such as plaited braid and ladder stitches, and also

applications of secondary fabric over padding or bits of carved wood. In Great Britain during the seventeenth century raised work, or stump work, as British raised work of this period is called now, was developed to a high degree of sophistication. Both amateur and professional needleworkers spun fantastic confections in three dimensions over the surfaces of cabinets for jewels, toilet articles or writing materials, mirror frames, pictures and a variety of objects (plate 48). European and biblical monarchs and other characters mingle with animals, reptiles, insects, birds and plants in settings showing tiny buildings and landscapes, the whole worked with silks, beads, mica, purls, bits of knitted or woven fabric, all of fanciful elaboration. Leaves, petals of flowers, walls of tents and edges of curtains were worked wholly or partly as fabrics separate from the foundation, and one can actually lift the edges up into real space. As though to temper the exuberance of these virtuoso performances, other furnishing fabrics and pictures were worked flat in cross or tent stitch; these pieces have also survived in large numbers.

In the seventeenth century the British were to develop yet another form of needlework specifically their own—a form that sprang from a love of the countryside and woodlands, a taste figuring prominently in the history of British art. From about 1650 through the first part of the next century, women worked bed hangings (curtains and valances) on a special twill-weave, linen-warp, cotton-weft foundation fabric with a napped surface that looked rather like flannel. We believe that this is the fabric they called *fustian*. On this foundation housewives—and probably some professional needleworkers also—embroidered patterns of twisting tree trunks and large-leafed branches swirling in abstract space or rising from hillocks or rockeries where creatures of many breeds cavort. Other hangings showed individual trees, animals and human figures arranged in irregular rows. All these motifs were worked in loosely plied long-staple worsted yarns (or crewels), either in shades of green (now usually faded to blue) or in a combination of colors (plate 49).

During the first half of the eighteenth century British needleworkers lavished special attention on canvas work for pictures, furniture covers, firescreens and floor carpets (plate 51). It was in this period that British needlework rejoined the mainstream of Western tradition. Silk and crewel embroideries continued to display superb workmanship, and white work in linen or cotton appeared more frequently, but the patterns are harder to identify as being specifically British.

As for the beginnings of the American tradition, unfortunately only a few of the first embroideries that were worked in the New World by European settlers in the seventeenth century have come down to us. Consequently, we must rely on portraits and documents to tell us how these early colonizers used needlework to dress and furnish their houses. Other than adopting whatever needlework tradi-

Colorplate 8.
The use of sculptured pile stitches has given the flowers, fruits and birds in this Berlin-work panel from a Victorian firescreen a tactile appeal. Probably American, about 1830–50. Height: 73 cm. (28¾ in.). Cooper-Hewitt Museum, gift of Mrs. Edgar S. Auchincloss, 1947

tions they may have found among the indigenous people, the first settlers had no choice but to look to the traditions of the homeland. In the southern and western parts of the continent settlers from Spain and France continued their own national traditions, and in the parts of the east and north that were not primarily British, pockets of Dutch, Germans and Scandinavians continued theirs. But the majority of the work that has survived from the seventeenth and eighteenth centuries comes from the British settlements along the East Coast, where the British, too, followed their own traditions.

Girls who were old enough to make samplers in England before they came to America (eight to ten years of age was not considered too young) brought their work with them. At least five such pieces survive today, one dating from about 1610–15, worked by Anne Gower and preserved in the Essex Institute, Salem, Massachusetts; one worked by Elizabeth Rush in 1675, now at the East Hampton (New York) Historical Society; and three others datable to the second half of the seventeenth century. Still three other samplers worked in precisely the same style (and all essentially like the English example of 1678 in plate 4, see page 12) were made in New England. They were the work of Loara Standish (daughter of Captain Miles Standish), about 1631–35, now in Pilgrim Hall in Plymouth; of Mary Hollingsworth, about 1658–60, in the Essex Institute; and of Sarah Lord, 1668, in a private collection.

Two rare New England embroideries of the seventeenth century are especially noteworthy. One is an embroidered picture of Esther and Ahasuerus signed and dated on the back by Rebekah Wheeler of Concord, Massachusetts, in 1664; it is now at the Concord Antiquarian Society. The other is an embroidered cabinet that was worked by Mary and Elizabeth Leverett about 1665. The girls were born in Boston, spent seven years in England with their parents, and then

47.
Fanciful country landscapes full of spirited creatures border this table carpet. English, about 1600. Width: 176 cm. (69 in.). Detail. Victoria and Albert Museum, London, National Art Collections Fund, 1928

48.
Set inside the lid of this rare and intricate cabinet (above, closed; below, open) is a portrait of a woman modeled in wax. The box is covered with satin-weave silk worked with colored silk yarns, couched silver and gilt purl and seed pearls. Stump work decorates the outer surface. English, 1650–1700. Height: 36 cm. (14¼ in.). Museum of Fine Arts, Boston, gift of Mrs. Elizabeth Learned Peabody, 1959

48

48

49.
Large-leafed flowering branches sprawl over this rich ensemble of bed hangings; at the base are hillocks representing the earth. English, 1675–1725. Height of curtains: 217 cm. (85½ in.). Height of valance (excluding modern fringe): 28 cm. (11 in.). Museum of Fine Arts, Boston, curtains purchased with the Textile Income Purchase Fund, 1960; valance, gift of Mrs. Samuel Cabot, 1961

50.
The Bradstreet family of Boston preserved this set of bed hangings showing a typical pattern of graceful flowering branches. American, 1725–50. Height of curtains (average): 218 cm. (86 in.). Height of valances (average): 24 cm. (9½ in.). Museum of Fine Arts, Boston, gift of Samuel Bradstreet, 1919

51.
The pattern of this exuberant floor carpet exploits the decorative value of various colorful garden blooms. English, signed with initials EN (or EM or EW?) and dated 1743. Length: 284.5 cm. (112 in.). Metropolitan Museum of Art, New York, gift of Irwin Untermyer, 1962

51

52

53

54

52.
Deer romp and rest on this chair-seat cover, one of a group of seven similar covers that were handed down in the Bradstreet family with the bed hangings illustrated in plate 50. American, 1725–50. Depth front to back: 40.5 cm. (16 in.). Museum of Fine Arts, Boston, gift of Samuel Bradstreet, 1924

53.
Worked by Sarah Tyler of Boston, this canvas-work chair-seat cover, embroidered mainly in tent stitch with colored crewels, was made as an upholstery fabric to be mounted directly on the seat. American, about 1740. Depth front to back, as originally framed: 56 cm. (22 in.). Metropolitan Museum of Art, New York, gift of R. Thornton Wilson, 1943, in memory of Florence Ellsworth Wilson

54.
The embroidered band at the hemline of this New England petticoat was visible only when the wearer lifted the edge of her gown, or as she walked. American, 1740–60. Circumference of band: about 248 cm. (97½ in.). Museum of Fine Arts, Boston, gift of Mrs. Samuel Cabot, 1938

returned to New England, where it is believed they worked the cabinet, perhaps with materials and patterns brought from England. It is now in the Essex Institute.

We have a number of records indicating that New Englanders got needlework patterns from England. In 1687 Judge Samuel Sewall of Boston wrote to England on behalf of his wife for the contemporary equivalent of an embroidery kit, complete with patterned foundation fabrics and a measured supply of crewels: "white Fustian drawn, enough for curtains, wallen [valance], counterpaine for a bed, and half a duz. chairs, with four threeded green worsted to work it."

The Sewall bed furnishings—if they were ever made—must have looked very much like the set of crewel-embroidered bed hangings bearing the initials AP and the date 1674 at the Society for the Preservation of New England Antiquities in Boston. They have a fustian foundation worked with two shades of green yarn in the then-typical English pattern of undulating branches with large leaves.

Some twenty years after work presumably began on the Sewall bed hangings and chair covers, Mrs. Richard Fifield of Boston embarked on the arduous task of embroidering another set of bed hangings using fustian (with the pattern already drawn on it) and crewels that her husband had brought her from England. The bed curtains were handed down in the family, and two of them are now in the Museum of Fine Arts, Boston. These embroideries, which are among the earliest-known crewel embroideries worked in this country, utilize not only British materials and patterns but also stitches that appear in similar work done in England—satin, long and short, chain and a variety of fancy filling stitches.

The flowering tree pattern in the Fifield curtains is first cousin to the bolder pattern decorating the English bed hangings in plate 49. A bit later—around 1725—a variation developed that seems to have continued in fashion, along with the main version of the pattern, into the middle of the century in both England and the colonies. The contorted trunk and branches become slimmer, flatten their curves and drop most of their leaves and flowers. The hillocks at the base and the animals cavorting in them all but disappear. More foundation fabric shows than crewels, and the color is light and airy. The bed hangings passed down in the Bradstreet family of Boston are a classic example of this style (plate 50). Unlike their English counterparts, which were worked largely in satin and long and short stitches, these New England curtains were worked mainly in self-couching (similar to Romanian) and flat stitches. Throughout most of the century these two stitches were favored in New England in this kind of work, probably because they place most of the yarn on the face of the fabric, thereby saving expensive yarns. Seven chair-seat covers preserved with the Bradstreet curtains by the same family have the same materials and

55.
Roses, carnations and other flowers are celebrated in this bed curtain that belonged to the Wade family of Ipswich, Massachusetts. American, 1740–60. Height: 216 cm. (85⅛ in.). Museum of Fine Arts, Boston, gift of Mrs. Jason Westerfield, 1959

stitches but depict landscapes rather than trees alone (plate 52). Related landscapes with trees and animals recur on bed valances and petticoat borders during the first half of the century (plate 54).

In addition to the two main classes of patterns represented by the Bradstreet curtains and the petticoat border, other groups of patterns —always floral—appear on eighteenth-century American furnishing fabrics. Some bed curtains, counterpanes and valances have staggered rows of floral sprigs or plants and trees loosely surrounded by flowering vines (plate 55). A shift in taste seems to have occurred as the century advanced, and it has been suggested that the more rigidly placed and the more stylized the floral elements appear, the later they are, some as late as 1770 (the Mary Breed embroideries in the Metropolitan Museum of Art) and perhaps even later. Another pattern system shows vinelike plants with short stems; these also date from the later part of the century. Some of the blue and white embroideries closely allied to these in design and workmanship have dates worked into the fabric—all within the 1760s or 1770s. Patterns on a few blue and white embroideries were worked with crewels (plate 103, see page 116), but the majority employed linen or cotton yarns in several shades of blue.

While the American embroideries of this kind worked in the first half of the century have foundation fabrics of fustian (napped twill, with linen warp and cotton wefts), the later pieces usually have plain-weave foundations that are not napped but have either all linen yarns or linen warp and cotton wefts.

In doing their silk embroidery, quilting, white work and canvas work, women in British America also continued the traditions of the mother country, and we have not yet identified stylistic or technical criteria to help distinguish an American group as such. The patterns, stitches, materials and workmanship in examples like those in plate 53 and colorplate 9 do not in themselves fix the work as American but only more generally as British. Undoubtedly, similar work was being done in Ireland, Scotland, Wales and other regions where British traditions were important.

Women in eighteenth-century America did not limit their embroidery to bed furnishings, chair-seat covers and petticoat borders. They also worked covers for gaming tables, panels for firescreens, pictures (including coats of arms and chimneypieces), workbags, dresses, pockets (to be tied around the waist under a woman's skirt), pocketbooks, christening blankets, stomachers, aprons, shoes, petticoats and men's caps (plates 56–58). Nor can the list be closed there, for at any time embroideries of other kinds may come to light.

Since we know that professional needleworkers of both sexes were active in the colonies and that the richest materials were available to anyone who had the price, those who entertain the notion that "early

Colorplate 9.
Scratched on the glass that covered this New England embroidered picture in its original frame was the inscription, "Wrought by Sarah Henshaw AD 1753." The picture, *King David and the Hanging of Absalom*, portrays, from left to right, King David on his throne, the death of his son Absalom, and David playing his harp. American, 1753. Height: 57.3 cm. (22½ in.). Museum of Fine Arts, Boston, Otis Norcross Fund, 1941

Colorplate 10.
Inscribed on the tomb in the center of this embroidered memorial picture are the words "In memory of Mrs. Susannah Chandler. Died August 28th 1811. Aged 56 years." These words, as well as the flesh portions, the sky and the mountains, are painted on the silk foundation; the other forms are embroidered. American, worked by Mary B. Tirrell, 1817. Height: 22 cm. (8⅝ in.). Cooper-Hewitt Museum, 1974

American" needlework is amateurish or provincial should promptly abandon it.

Two other widespread misconceptions exist; the first is that window curtains were embroidered with crewels during the seventeenth and eighteenth centuries. Although in recent years crewel embroideries—some eighteenth-century originals, some reproductions—have been hung at the windows in some restored American interiors, no evidence indicates that this sort of needlework was in fact used to cover windows in eighteenth-century America. Possibly some homemaker of the time did so as a matter of personal taste, but there was no general fashion for it.

The second widespread misconception is that Turkey work was made with a needle. Most historians now agree that true Turkey work—a coarse pile fabric resembling a knotted rug—was made on a small rug loom and patterned with pile knots that were tied on the warp during the weaving process rather than looped with a needle. To compound the problem, however, there actually was a form of needlework called "Turkey work." An advertisement of 1716 in the *Boston News-Letter*, listing a number of kinds of fancy work that were to be taught at a certain house, includes "Turkey-work for Hand-kerchiefs two ways." Since the carpetlike fabric we have described as Turkey work could not have been used for handkerchiefs, it is clear that the Turkey work being advertised was something else entirely, perhaps a form of the fine embroidery on linen and silk that was practiced at the time in most parts of the Ottoman Empire.

Until recently many writers mistakenly grouped under the headings "Turkey work" and "rug hooking" yet another class of needleworked fabrics that American women produced in the eighteenth and nine-

56.
Known as the "Bourne Heirloom," this canvas-work chimneypiece was made by the wife of Colonel Sylvanus Bourne of Massachusetts. The popular "fishing lady" motif, flanked by other figures, appears in the center of a charming New England setting. American, mid-eighteenth century. Height of image within frame: 52 cm. (20½ in.). Museum of Fine Arts, Boston, Seth Kettell Sweetser Fund, 1921

57.
Elegant eighteenth-century embroidered gentlemen's caps like this example from New England were descendants of earlier fine headgear worn at home by English gentlemen (see plate 8). American, 1725–50. Height including finial: 33 cm. (13 in.). Museum of Fine Arts, Boston, gift of Mary Whiton Hutchinson, 1961

58.
In eighteenth-century America both men and women carried pocketbooks like this. On the lining is a cross-stitched inscription: "This was rought by me Ruth Twitchel in the year 1793 &c." The little canvas-work purse was probably made in New England. Height (folded): 13.5 cm. (5¼ in.). Museum of Fine Arts, Boston, gift of Mrs. Luke Vincent Lockwood, 1941

56

teenth centuries and called "bed rugs." Almost all these originated in Connecticut and share a number of common characteristics, including patterns with a flowering vine framing a central plant, initials and a date (plate 60). The technique involves neither rug knotting nor hooking but random needle (running) stitches worked with heavy wool yarns pulled up into loops through a heavy wool foundation, after which some of the loops are clipped to form a cut-and-uncut pile surface.

For a variety of reasons—economic, social, political—by the early years of the nineteenth century young women in America as well as in Great Britain were working their needles in ways different from their grandmothers'. Bright printed textiles had become easily available, and since they were relatively cheap they were substituted for many household furnishings previously worked by needle. It was no longer necessary for women to spend years working on a set of bed hangings or furniture covers, as earlier generations had. For example, the woman who initialed (MM) and dated two narrow crewel-embroidered bed curtains now at Colonial Williamsburg worked on them from November 3, 1701, until an unspecified day in the week of August 21, 1702; and although it is possible that she also embroidered more pieces for her bed during that time, it seems likely that she took the ten months just to decorate the two curtains she inscribed. Simply to draw out the pattern on the foundation of a large textile took considerable time, even for a professional draftsman. Walter Gale, a schoolmaster working in Sussex, England, in the middle of the eighteenth century, noted in his diary that it took him five days of "close application" to draw the pattern on a bed quilt.

Also by the early years of the nineteenth century, more and more

57

58

59

girls were attending more schools where they were taught needlework. They continued to toil over samplers, costume embroideries, carpets and other utilitarian pieces, but they also made other things. During the late eighteenth and early nineteenth centuries the most noteworthy new works they turned out were the numerous silk-embroidered pictures depicting children dressed as shepherds and shepherdesses, allegorical, biblical and historical scenes, still-life pieces (plate 59) and the even more numerous mourning pieces that record the passing of a national figure, a relative or some other loved one (colorplate 10). Embroidered maps, made as samplers, prove that schoolgirls learned more than just technique as they plied their needles (plate 61). Young girls also worked pictures in imitation of engravings or etchings (plate 62). These nineteenth-century pictures and samplers survive in quantity today. Even sailors embroidered pictures during the nineteenth century, using wool yarns and—naturally enough—depicting sailing vessels. British seamen of the period are particularly associated with the work, for they seem to have practiced the art of embroidering pictures as nineteenth-century American sailors practiced the art of carving or incising patterns on ivory from sea mammals (scrimshaw).

for her dower chest. Initialed RH and dated 1776. Length: 231 cm.(91¼ in.). Smithsonian Institution, National Museum of History and Technology, deposited by Nancy Kendrew Bell

61.
England and Wales (with "Part of Scotland," as a section at the top reads) were rendered by Elizabeth Evennett as a school sampler. English, dated July 17, 1801. Height: 57 cm. (22½ in.). Cooper-Hewitt Museum, bequest of Mrs. Henry E. Coe, 1941

60

61

Many young American women turned their excellent school training to practical use when they set up their homes. Some of them were ambitious enough to work large floor carpets. Among the important surviving examples is the drawing-room carpet from the home of Judge Pliny Moore in Champlain, New York (plate 63). Judge Moore's two daughters, Ann and Sophia, joined forces with Harriett Hicks to work the cross-stitch carpet and a smaller hearth rug and stair carpet to match. They began the project in 1808 and finished in 1812. Zeruah Higley Guernsey of Castleton, Vermont, spent almost five years on a large floor carpet, and when she finished, she worked the date, 1835, into the pattern (plate 64). Unlike the Moore-Hicks carpet with its canvas ground and cross stitches, this later example shows chain stitches defining the pattern on a foundation of coarse wool.

Although regional styles persisted in some parts of North America during the nineteenth century, the growth of cities, of transportation, of public education and of magazines all operated to draw the attention of American women to international fashions coming from London and Paris. American needlework became increasingly sophisticated, more an international art than a national one. In every American

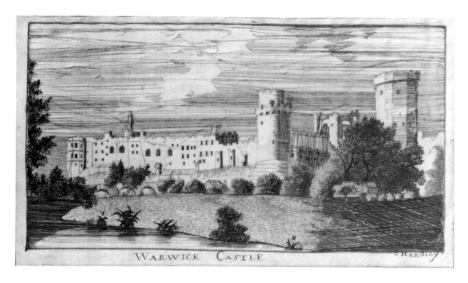

WARWICK CASTLE

62.
In embroidered pictures made in imitation of prints, like this one of Warwick Castle signed by S. Handley, the yarns were manipulated to enhance the resemblance of the stitched lines to engraved or etched lines. English or American, about 1790–1810. Height: 27.4 cm. (10¾ in.). Cooper-Hewitt Museum, gift of Mrs. H. P. Davison, 1974

city or village, women who could afford it bought or rented needlework patterns published abroad—available either as separate sheets or bound into the influential ladies' magazines of the day, like *Godey's Lady's Book* and *Peterson's Magazine*, from which women derived inspiration in so many aspects of their lives.

From about 1830 to about 1870, American and European women alike were gripped by one of the longest-lived fads in needlework—Berlin work. In the Berlin-work patterns, which were printed on graphlike checked paper, each square represented a stitch—usually a tent or cross stitch—and the pattern was defined by symbols or colors placed in certain squares. The embroiderer transferred the pattern to the canvas by counting squares on the pattern and placing the stitches on the canvas at the corresponding warp/weft intersections. The firm of A. Philipson began publishing this kind of pattern in Berlin about 1804, and a few years later the L. W. Wittich firm, also in Berlin, began issuing the patterns with colored marks rather than engraved symbols to designate the colors. Firms in Vienna and Paris, as well as other firms in Germany, sprang up to answer the spreading demand for Berlin work. With the technical aids that Berlin work offered, almost anyone could produce needlework fantasies. The subjects of the patterns ranged from still lifes and floral and animal subjects to sentimental figure subjects and copies of popular paintings. Over a period of some forty years different kinds of wool, usually heavier than the crewels of the eighteenth century, and special kinds of canvases appeared on the market to be sold in connection with the Berlin-work patterns, and dealers did a thriving business in silk yarns and beads as well.

Every sort of useful object, and many frivolous ones, that could be decorated with needlework inspired Berlin-work patterns: upholstery fabrics, pillow covers, valances, table covers, suspenders, bellpulls, coverlets, firescreens, purses, belts, pincushions—it would be hard to compile a complete list. The surface of the finished needlework might be relatively flat, showing two kinds of stitches of the same or nearly the same size, a combination of large and small stitches of the same kind, or any other combination plus areas of sculptured pile (color-plate 8, see page 54) and beads, or surfaces covered entirely with pile or beads.

The nineteenth century has also left us many examples of a totally different kind of needlework. Thanks to their early training, many women acquired the skill needed to work fine cotton and linen for everyday use, so the Berlin-work years are also the years of delicate cut-fabric work, withdrawn-element work and deflected-element embroidery—all of which involve removing or rearranging the threads of the ground for decorative effects—as well as eyelet embroidery, hemstitching and the entire vocabulary of refined, small-scale white

63.
Ann and Sophia Moore and Harriett Hicks jointly cross-stitched this floor carpet with brown, green and white wool yarns. The lower edge was shaped to fit around the hearth. American, 1808–12. Length: 478 cm. (188 in.). Metropolitan Museum of Art, New York, gift of Isabelle C. Mygatt, 1923

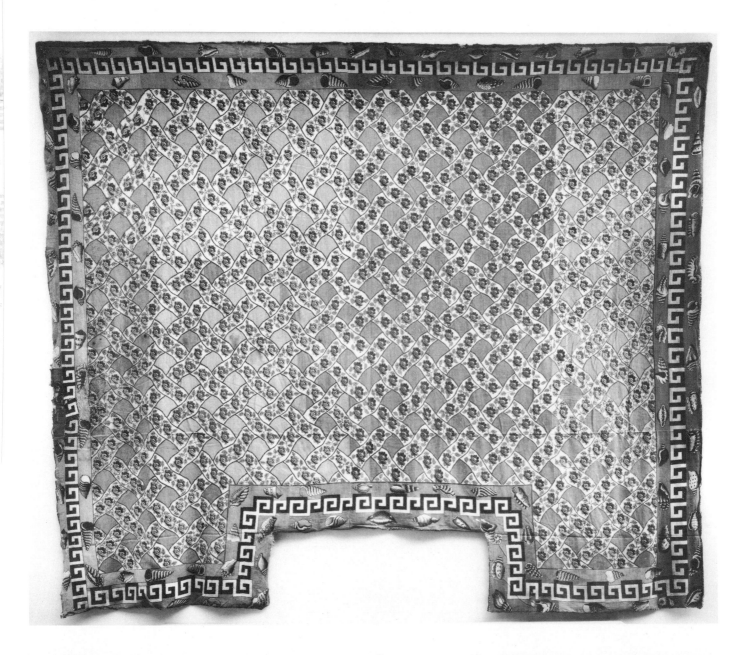

work. Toward the end of the century this taste for refinement fell victim to the growing public worship of mechanical precision as the world was turned upside down by the power of machines. In Europe and America people accepted the great international expositions presenting technological and industrial developments as arbiters of taste, and women (and possibly men and children, too) disciplined their hands to perform with the cold exactness of machines. Incredible tours de force of precision needlework, especially white work, came into being (plate 65).

In reaction to this dehumanizing of handiwork, during the last half of the nineteenth century numbers of arts and crafts movements sprang up in Europe and America. In England the movement was spearheaded by the versatile William Morris—writer, designer and political theorist—who asserted that the decorative arts should reflect the spirit of nature and the qualities of handcraft rather than remaining slave to the limitations of machine mass production. With a small group of colleagues, he set up business in London in 1861 to design and execute furniture, wall coverings and all sorts of textiles (plate 66). Many Pre-Raphaelite artists joined in championing the cause by designing for Morris's firm, but it is the younger group active in the Royal School of Art Needlework in London from 1872 onward that

64.
Besides the initials of the maker, Zeruah Higley Guernsey (later Caswell), this colorful chain-stitched wool floor carpet bears the initials of two Potawatomi Indian medical students who are believed to have boarded with the Guernsey family. American, dated 1835. Length: 407 cm. (160 in.). Metropolitan Museum of Art, New York, gift of Katherine Keyes, 1938, in memory of her father, Homer Eaton Keyes

65.
In this center section of an extraordinary table cover, three cupids are surrounded by representations of the Four Seasons taken from seventeenth- or eighteenth-century French designs. European, perhaps Belgian or Swiss, about 1890–1920. Length (format almost square): 81.9 cm. (32¼ in.). Detail. Honolulu Academy of Arts, gift of Mrs. Charles M. Cooke, 1927

65

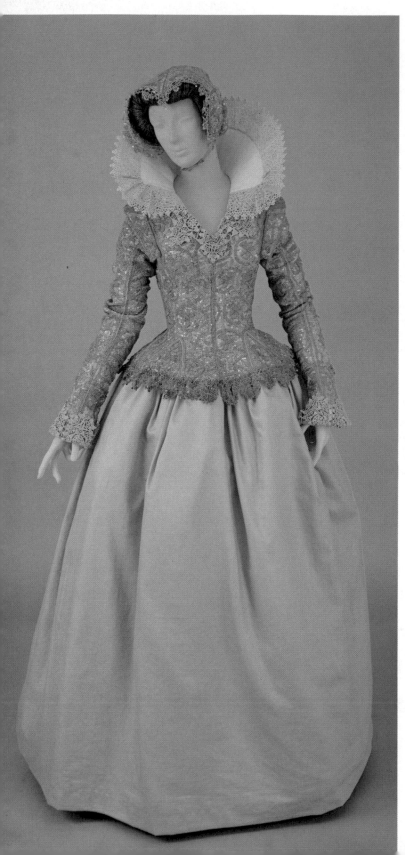

COLORPLATE 12

COLORPLATE 11

deserves the honors for establishing "art needlework." In America, sympathetic decorative artists, particularly Louis Comfort Tiffany and Candace Wheeler, supported the same artistic attitudes and tastes. As a result, throughout the last quarter of the nineteenth century and the first quarter of the next, professional needleworkers—as well as ladies who might have settled for Berlin work twenty years earlier—were working in the new idiom, which incorporated elements of medieval, Renaissance and Oriental styles and echoes of new styles that were developing in continental Europe (colorplate 12). The most pervasive of these new directions, Art Nouveau, quickly spread throughout Europe and America, and adherents of the new ornamental style applied its forms—essentially languorous plant shapes—to everything from furniture to textiles (plate 67).

No history of the main Western traditions would be complete without mention of one class of embroideries Americans developed to a high level of refinement—the applied-work and pieced-work quilted bedcovers we know as quilts. Great Britain is once more the source of inspiration, and patchwork quilts made in Britain in the eighteenth century are indistinguishable from the same kind of quilt made in America. But in time American women, and some men and children also, developed the art to new heights of fancy and variety.

One group of American quilts close to the British prototype achieved dazzling optical effects through the piecing of small, angular bits of plain or printed fabric. During the nineteenth century the motifs took geometrical shapes: squares, triangles, hexagons, long narrow rectangles, stars and circles. After a while the quiltmakers seem to have tired of these perfect shapes, and toward the end of the century they began to cut shapes willy-nilly and piece them together with no apparent logic; these became known as crazy quilts. As though to compound the madness, needleworkers used the most garish plain and patterned silks they could find, and further embellished the surface with stitchery executed in every kind of fancy glossy, textured yarn, representing every kind of thing made by man or nature (colorplate 13).

In or around 1850 friends and relatives of one Benoni Pearce of Pawling, New York, made and signed eighty-one pieced- and applied-work squares that form the top of a quilted bedcover assembled in honor of her engagement (plate 68). Because they were made from pieces worked by well-wishers, coverlets of this kind were known as friendship quilts. This is only one of dozens of types of quilted coverlets that have come down to us from nineteenth-century America. Some of them, like the Bible quilts that Harriet Powers, a freed slave, made in Athens, Georgia, transcend the limitations of utilitarian objects. Profound and personal works of art, the Powers quilts are as powerful spiritually as they are naive artistically (plate 69).

Colorplate 11.
Floral motifs cover this richly worked waistcoat and coif. On the linen foundation a variety of raised and couching stitches are enhanced by the use of silver and gilt yarns and spangles. English, about 1575–1610. Museum of Fine Arts, Boston, Elizabeth Day McCormick Collection, 1943

Colorplate 12.
Created in the art needlework idiom, this velvet evening bag displays a dazzling beaded peacock. The gilt-metal frame and chain were designed from a print in the collection of the Cooper Union Museum. American, about 1910–15. Height: 24 cm. (9½ in.). Cooper-Hewitt Museum, gift of Gwendolyn Sauvage, 1956

66

A unique and fascinating quilt form developed in Hawaii, where the wives of American missionaries began teaching quilting techniques to native women about 1820. Hawaiian women soon invented variations on the patterns brought from the mainland. The symmetrical floral and snowflake shapes took on a tropical air (plate 70), and local motifs crept in. Native women jealously guarded the privilege of developing their own patterns and giving them names. In these covers the quilting stitches follow the shapes of pattern outlines rather than an abstract system of squares or circles. Toward the end of the nineteenth century Hawaiian women made quilts depicting human figures, with inscriptions, and still others displayed the flag and coat of arms of the kingdom of Hawaii.

Finally, in this brief survey of Western needlework, we come to the delightful world of provincial embroidery. To appreciate its special character, we have to imagine a world without television, radio, air travel, cars and—until a hundred and fifty years or so ago, and in some places much less—railroads. We have to think of pockets of people living on mountaintops, in isolated valleys, in villages separated from one another by vast expanses of water or wilderness. These people lived on the land and its bounty. Most of them had heard about kings and courts, splendid palaces and great cities; but only those few who lived near them ever saw any of these splendors, and none could afford to emulate them. But human nature is what it is, and people everywhere love color, texture, dressing up and decorating their homes. Over a matter of centuries people living in rural or isolated areas developed means of achieving these goals as best they could, using materials they could make, barter for or, if they were fortunate, buy. What they thought looked good was what their ancestors had thought looked good. When direct contact with the great world outside became easier, people in rural areas developed a taste for its novelties—as evidenced by the representations of cars filling up at a gas station or the words "Coca-Cola" that have appeared in recent years on applied-work shirt fronts (*molas*) from the islands bordering the Gulf of San Blas off Panama. Once this happened, local traditions weakened and in many places died out. Provincial cultures of which needlework traditions are a major part have survived only if they are fortunate enough to have members who are proud of their heritage and act to preserve or revive their traditions—or if they attract outsiders who seek to achieve the same goal.

Throughout Europe, in sophisticated as well as in simpler cultures, needlework traditions reveal both a distant echo of the national urban culture and also a vigorous local style. We have chosen for illustration only a few examples of regional European embroidery, specifically some of those that display a pronounced national or cultural style as opposed to the far greater number whose formal vocabularies are almost interchangeable.

66.
William Morris designed this embroidered hanging, using motifs that recall medieval and Renaissance fabrics while also reflecting new trends in contemporary design. English, about 1875–80. Height: 214 cm. (84¼ in.). Victoria and Albert Museum, London

67.
Hector Guimard, who designed the Art Nouveau entrances to the Paris Métro, designed this silk and tulle dress fabric worked in stem, chain and knotted stitches, cutwork and faggoting. French, about 1906–7. Height: 68 cm. (26¾ in.). Cooper-Hewitt Museum, gift of Mrs. Hector Guimard, 1949

67

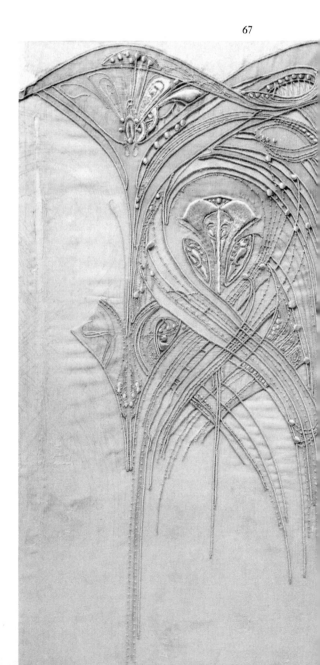

Colorplate 13.
Worked by Pauline Rilling in San Antonio, Texas, in 1888, this witty crazy quilt won first prize in the textile section of the San Antonio International Exposition of that year. Height: 218 cm. (86 in.). San Antonio Museum Association (Witte Memorial Museum), gift of Mrs. Adolph Grasso, 1952

68.
Benoni Pearce's dazzling friendship quilt, made for her engagement, is worked with pieced and applied cottons, embroidery stitches, pen work and quilting. American, dated 1850. Length (square format): 262 cm. (103 in.). Smithsonian Institution, National Museum of History and Technology, gift of Adelaide Pearce Green and Mira Pearce Noyes Boorman, 1972

69.
Biblical subjects ranging from Adam and Eve to the Crucifixion ornament this applied-work cotton quilt designed and worked by Harriet Powers, a freed slave. American, 1886. Height: 187.3 cm. (73¾ in.). Smithsonian Institution, National Museum of History and Technology, gift of Mr. and Mrs. H. M. Heckman, 1969

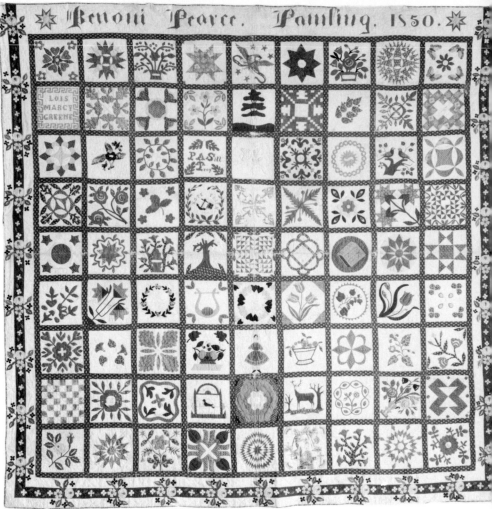

68

69

70

The regional needlework of Spain is particularly handsome and varied. Many parts of the country produced magnificent needleworked bedcovers and garments with flowers of many kinds, birds, beasts and human beings in subtle but brilliant color schemes that have an identity all their own. The black and white work of Salamanca is particularly distinctive (plate 72).

Polish regional embroidery is also enormously rich and diverse. The man's suit in plate 71—a costume to be worn on festive occasions—shows the typical style of Zakopane, a town in the Tatra Mountains region of the Carpathian range. It is particularly significant because it demonstrates a basic characteristic of most European regional needlework and costume: the tendency to preserve fashionable shapes and ornaments from earlier urban garments. In this case the prototype is an aggressively masculine one—the military uniform of certain French officers toward the end of the eighteenth century. We can see the inspiration for this suit in a portrait Gilbert Stuart painted in 1798 of the Vicomte de Noailles. In the portrait, the viscount's uniform has skintight breeches trimmed over the thighs with the same kind of braidwork that has survived in shape, if not in color and material, in the trousers of the Polish suit, which dates from the early years of the twentieth century. Curiously, neither the cut nor the ornamentation of the coat bears any resemblance to the military costume that served as prototype for the trousers.

The needlework of Russia is as extensive and heterogeneous as the many peoples that make up the country. Illustrating a relatively

70.
The pattern in this bedcover from the Hawaiian Islands is called *Ka Ua Kani Lehua* (The Rain That Rustles Lehua Blossoms). Yellow cotton motifs are applied to a red foundation and quilted in lines conforming to the shapes of the motifs, a procedure typical of Hawaiian work. 1875–1900. Length: 213.4 cm. (84 in.). Honolulu Academy of Arts, gift of Damon Giffard, 1959

71.
When they dressed for festivals, men in rural parts of Europe, like their women, wore brilliant primary colors. A typical example is this Polish festival suit in which all the embroidered motifs are brightly colored. Early twentieth century. Metropolitan Museum of Art, New York, Costume Institute, gift of the J. L. Hudson Company, 1944

72.
Familiar motifs in Spanish regional needlework—the double-headed eagle, birds and tulips—figure in the black embroidery on this sleeve from a Salamancan woman's blouse. Spanish, nineteenth century. Length: 69 cm. (27⅛ in.). Cooper-Hewitt Museum, gift of Mary B. Nesmith, 1961

71

72

sophisticated strain of regional work, our example (plate 73) shows a linen border from a sheet on which double-headed crowned eagles, once a symbol of the imperial czars, alternate wth peacocks. Like the regional needlework of most Central and Eastern European cultures, Russian work generally has geometric motifs rather than the relatively elaborate forms in the linen border illustrated. Geometric patterning depended on counted-thread techniques, which allowed the embroiderer to transfer the pattern to the foundation without having to draw it out first on the fabric, as was done in the case of the border.

The Scandinavian cultures have given us a large and rich body of regional needlework. Among the most admired types is the white work of Denmark, Norway and Sweden; a Danish example is given here (plate 74). In Denmark, white work goes under the generic name *hvidsøm* (literally, "white seam" or "white stitch"), and among the various kinds of *hvidsøm* produced in the past is the work of women living in the moorlands near Copenhagen. Their embroideries are often referred to as *hedebo* (literally, "moor dweller") work. Most of the Danish white work we have today dates from the eighteenth or nineteenth century. In working it, the needleworker used withdrawn-element work, cut-fabric work and deflected-element embroidery to achieve the open effect; chain, satin and buttonhole stitches served for most of the ornamental work. Like much other regional work, this was used for household linens, particularly towels and bed linens, and also for personal linens, especially the contents of a bride's dower chest.

73.
Imperial Russian eagles, double headed and crowned, mingle with plump peacocks on this linen border of a sheet. The border is worked with deflected-element embroidery and with gilt and black silk yarns in chain stitch. Russian, probably nineteenth century. Height including fringe: 28 cm. (11 in.). Detail. Cooper-Hewitt Museum, Au Panier Fleuri Fund, 1954

74.
Danish white work of the type called
hvidsøm combines openwork with a
variety of ornamental stitches, as in this
beautifully executed towel. Danish, dated
1838. Height: 99 cm. (39 in.). Detail.
Metropolitan Museum of Art, New York,
Rogers Fund, 1948

COLORPLATE 14

COLORPLATE 15

4 Mainstreams in the East

To the Western mind, schooled in different religions, visual styles and attitudes toward materials, Eastern needlework is an exotic art, profoundly attractive but alien. Oriental beliefs and institutions gave rise to images and needleworked objects that tantalize the Western viewer because they resemble familiar things but have unfamiliar meanings when viewed in the Eastern context. The ceremonial cover, or rumal, of India, for example, to the Western eye should be a small table cover, but it is not. The sumptuous Japanese kimono fabrics should be sections of paintings, but they are not. Because they are so unfamiliar and so rich in ways that Western embroideries are not, examples of Oriental needlework conjure up all the glamour and mystery of the East.

We know that decorative needlework was practiced in China at least one, and possibly two, thousand years before the beginning of the Christian Era in the West. Traces of an embroidered fabric are preserved in the patina of a bronze urn dating from the Shang dynasty (c. 1523–1028 B.C.), and a literary reference earlier than the eighth century B.C. mentions the interrelations of painting and embroidery. The earliest embroidered textiles we have from the Far East were found in Scythian tombs in the Altai Mountains in Siberia near the Mongolian border. Among the fabrics found in the tombs, which date from the fifth to fourth centuries B.C., is an embroidered silk showing birds and plants and also some pieced and applied work. Other excavations in Siberia have yielded embroidered gauze and damask fabrics. From the sixth to tenth centuries A.D. we have great embroidered Buddhist hangings with celestial and human figures and flowers worked in silk and couched gilt yarns.

As in Europe, the art of needlework in Asia eventually came to imitate the art of painting. Superb examples of this kind of work dating from the tenth century and later still exist. They are so delicately executed that at first one cannot be sure that they are not in fact

Colorplate 14.
The wild goose on this Chinese rank badge was the emblem of a civil official of the fourth rank. The badge would be sewn on a dragon coat worn on ceremonial occasions. Chinese, Ch'ing dynasty, eighteenth or nineteenth century. Height: 28.4 cm. (11¼ in.). Cooper-Hewitt Museum, gift of the Estate of Mrs. Robert H. Patterson, 1941

Colorplate 15.
The exquisitely rendered pattern on this Taoist priest's robe represents the universe with both literal and symbolic images. The foundation—barely visible at the edges—is black silk completely covered with embroidery. Chinese, Ch'ing dynasty, nineteenth century. Cooper-Hewitt Museum, gift of Harvey Smith, 1968

76

75

75.
An eighteenth-century Chinese court lady of high rank wore this imperial dragon robe of gauze-weave silk worked with couched gilt yarns and upright Gobelin stitches in colored silks. Chinese, Ch'ing dynasty, Ch'ien-lung period (1736–95). Metropolitan Museum of Art, New York, gift of Marian Hague, 1943

76.
Philippine pineapple fiber cloth (piña cloth) worked with pineapple yarn was used to make this scarf or long cover, one end of which is shown here. Nineteenth century. Length: 244 cm. (96 in.). Detail. Metropolitan Museum of Art, New York, gift of Mrs. H. McKnight Moore, in memory of her mother, Mrs. James Suydam, 1924

paintings, since the embroideries, like the paintings, were rendered on plain-weave silk foundations and since they show only a few strands of untwisted silk in each stitch, which might almost be part of the foundation itself. Under the Ming dynasty (1368–1644) touches of paint and ink were acceptable in embroideries of this kind. During the same period and later, needlework patterns on useful objects and garments displayed birds, insects, flowers, geometric shapes and human figures. Most of this work was done by ladies of the leisure class at home.

Apart from album leaves, hanging scrolls, screens, chair covers, mirror and fan cases, bed hangings, temple banners and badges signifying rank, the most familiar and impressive needlework from China has come to us in the form of embroidery on dragon robes. It was the Manchus, the northern people who established the Ch'ing dynasty (1644–1912), who developed the dragon robe. The color and ornamentation were strictly controlled from the imperial court, and all robes were made in imperial workshops. Since the regulations changed from time to time, we can date some of the robes fairly accurately.

Among the most handsome of all the surviving dragon robes are those bearing imperial symbols (plate 75). The specific choice of symbols varies according to the sex and rank of the owner, but all imperial dragon robes have five-clawed dragons, clouds (representing heaven), water (a double band at the bottom with wavy lines representing the sea with breaking surf) and mountains (representing earth) rising from the sea. Only a few robes also display the sacrificial emblems believed to have been reserved for the emperor himself for use on special occasions.

The example in plate 75, which was made for a woman of high rank in the imperial court—an empress, dowager empress or important imperial consort—dates from the Ch'ien-lung period (1736–95) and is worked with silk and gilt yarns on a foundation of silk gauze. The upright Gobelin stitches are neatly finished on the back and therefore render the pattern as clearly on the back of the fabric as on the front. Many other robes are worked on satin or other solid-weave silk foundations, and yet another group is made of fine silk tapestry weave rather than needlework.

Like the robes, the rank badges (popularly known as "mandarin squares") displayed symbols and shapes that were changed at times by decree, and they can be fairly well dated on that basis. The badges, which were either embroidered or tapestry woven, were sewn to the chest and upper back sections of dragon coats that were worn over the dragon robes on ceremonial occasions. Colorplate 14 shows a badge for a civil official of the fourth rank. Birds signified civil rank, and beasts indicated military rank (there were eight ranks for each of the two classes of government officials). The choice of elements

77.
On this shawl made in China for export to the West, full-blown flowers, birds and butterflies embroidered in brilliant silks stand out against the black ground. Knotted silk fringe trims the edges. Chinese, Ch'ing dynasty, 1875–1900. Length (including fringe): 210.5 cm. (83 in.). Detail. Metropolitan Museum of Art, New York, gift of Mrs. Lesley Frost Ballentine, in memory of Joseph W. Ballentine, 1975

78

78.
Eighteenth-century Japanese woodblock prints show kabuki actors in female roles, fashionable ladies and courtesans wearing kimonos made of elaborate fabrics like this. Japanese, Edo period, Meiwa era (1764–71). Height: 68.6 cm. (27 in.). Honolulu Academy of Arts, gift of Mrs. Charles Adams, 1932

79.
An imposing cock dominates this silk hanging worked with colored silks and silver and gilt yarns. Japanese, nineteenth century. Height: 198 cm. (78 in.). Metropolitan Museum of Art, New York, gift of Laura Wheeler, 1937

Colorplate 16.
Designed for a male actor playing a female role in the kabuki theater, this brilliant robe was a quick-change costume: the top portion could be inverted quickly to show a second outfit. Japanese, nineteenth century. Honolulu Academy of Arts, gift of Earle Ernst, 1951

79

and their composition suggest that this badge was made during the Ch'ing dynasty, but probably not earlier than the eighteenth or nineteenth century.

A relatively small number of embroidered priests' robes have come down to us. Robes for Buddhist priests were usually made of a patchwork of woven silks. It is the robes of Taoist priests that were characteristically richly embroidered (colorplate 15). Unlike Buddhist priests' robes, which are either simple rectangles or rectangles shaped at one end, Taoist robes are long rectangles (sometimes curved at the ends) with a slit running from one end to the center. This conformation allows the priest to wear the fabric over the shoulders like a poncho that is open down the front. The example shown here, which is one of the richest to have survived, has borders that seem to have been taken from a different robe and applied to this field. The main section, which is solidly covered with couched gilt yarns and glistens like a sheet of gold, shows the dragon, earth, water and heaven symbols that appear also on the imperial dragon robes and, in the middle of the back, below the collar, a symbolic representation of the universe.

Eighteenth- or early nineteenth-century Chinese needlework of this quality is seldom found outside museum collections. More recent embroideries of fine design and workmanship are of course more numerous. A characteristic example of fine Chinese needlework of the later nineteenth century is the woman's coat in colorplate 17. The coat is made of wool broadcloth with applied satin borders and sleeve bands, and the whole is embroidered with colored silk and gilt yarns and figured silk tape.

Trade between China and the West gave rise to a separate class of export work that reflects the tastes of both cultures. Silk-embroidered shawls with knotted fringe are probably the most familiar examples we have of the export textiles (plate 77). Long referred to as "Manila shawls," and at times exported through Manila, these embroideries were actually made in China. The shawls were worked with colored silk yarns on white or colored silk foundations or entirely in one color; in some examples there are representations of human figures with heads and hands of painted ivory or sculptured mother-of-pearl. They reached the height of fashion in the years just before and just after 1850, when women in the West wore shawls as cloaks. The shawls changed size and shape with dress fashions, the smaller square pieces dating from the earlier years, when slim dresses were in style, the larger oblong pieces dating from the years after 1850, when crinoline petticoats extended the area the shawl had to cover.

True Philippine embroidery intended for the Western market is quite different. Native workers used a local material, a fine plain-weave fabric made from fibers taken from pineapple leaves—piña cloth—and worked it mainly with openwork and satin and buttonhole

Colorplate 17.
This remarkable coat for a woman has a
foundation combining plain wool broadcloth with silk. Chinese, about 1850–1900.
Metropolitan Museum of Art, New York,
gift of Dorothy A. Gordon and Virginia
A. White, in memory of Madge Ashley,
1973

80

81

stitches. Girls trained in convent schools used the technique to make blouses, handkerchiefs and scarves or long covers like the one in plate 76. The patterns were derived from European sources and do not reflect indigenous textile traditions.

It seems reasonable to assume that Chinese needlework as an art traveled to Japan through Korea in the sixth century A.D., along with Chinese traditions in painting and sculpture, and that it fused with existing forms of Japanese embroidery. We know that during the Nara period (710–84) Japanese embroiderers produced pictures of Buddha and his attendants in chain and knotted stitches, stitches that were used in China at a very early period.

The earliest Japanese embroidered fabrics we have in any quantity are fragments of splendid kimonos that fashionable women wore during the Momoyama (1568–1600) and Tokugawa or Edo (1600–1867) periods. One of these fragments is shown in plate 78. This kimono fabric is worked in embroidery stitches in colored silks and gilt yarns on a prominently patterned silk-damask foundation. In many of the other surviving examples, needlework is combined with tie dyeing, resist dyeing, stenciling or pattern weaving to produce effects of extraordinary richness. These fragments also show examples of *kara-ori* weaving, a technique in which untwisted silk yarns float for some distance over the surface of the foundation fabric, resembling long satin stitches. One must study the back of such fabrics to determine whether passages like these were woven or embroidered.

80.
The intricate patterns that were later copied in the West, where they became known as "Paisley patterns," are embroidered rather than woven in this large red shawl from Kashmir. Indian, about 1850–60. Length: 184 cm. (72½ in.). Cooper-Hewitt Museum, gift of Marian Hague, 1946

81.
Professional needleworkers perhaps employed in an Indian court manufactory made this large cotton cover with graceful stylized motifs worked in colored silks and silver and gilt yarns and quilted with a herringbone pattern. Indian, Mughal style, late seventeenth–eighteenth century. Length: 328.5 cm. (129¼ in.). Museum of Fine Arts, Boston, gift of John Goelet, 1966

82.
With its sprightly depiction of hunts on foot and on horseback, this rumal from Chamba in the Himalayas served as an elegant gift wrapping. Indian, probably eighteenth century. Length: 81.3 cm. (32 in.). Metropolitan Museum of Art, New York, Rogers Fund, 1931

In later Japanese needlework, when the ground fabrics of garments were often plain, the placement of the ornament on the foundation is wonderfully subtle in itself even when the garment was intended for use in the theater and therefore very boldly patterned (colorplate 16). It is this exquisite sense of placement that seems to set Japanese work apart from other needlework of the East, and the same may be said for the ease and assurance with which Japanese needleworkers combined their techniques with other methods of decorating textiles. Japanese embroiderers also excelled at pictorial work, and even here their work shows a sensitivity to the purely decorative effect of materials and stitches as well as a concern for true representation (plate 79).

In India, no embroideries dating from before the sixteenth century survive. During the early part of that century the Mongols had made inroads in India, and Akbar the Great consolidated the Mughal Empire throughout northern India in the second half of the century. The Mughal court adopted the culture of Persia and with it Persian traditions in needlework. We have references to embroiderers working in ateliers at the court, and it was there that patterns like the fluidly symmetrical one seen in plate 81 were developed. Under the influence of the court an Indo-Persian style took shape, and needleworkers used it in decorating great covers and hangings, waistbands, turban cloths and other costume embroideries worked on cotton or silk with colored silks and gilt and silver yarns.

In rural parts of India and in regions that felt the influence of Mughal styles very little, embroiderers using a needle or small hook (the *ari*, for making rapid chain stitches) decorated furnishing and costume fabrics in several local styles. The needleworks of the Punjab,

82

83.
Quilted cotton bedcovers chain-stitched and fringed with yellow silk like this one were made by native embroiderers in Bengal for the Portuguese market. Indian, probably 1600–1625. Length (including fringe): 291.5 cm. (115 in.). Detail. Museum of Fine Arts, Boston, gift of Mrs. John Gardner Coolidge, 1946

COLORPLATE 18

COLORPLATE 19

Colorplate 18.
Worked in Sind, India, this head shawl is almost entirely covered with red and green silk embroidered floral motifs. Indian, nineteenth or early twentieth century. Length: 125 cm. (49¼ in.). Detail. Cooper-Hewitt Museum, gift of C. Albert Jacob, Jr., 1957

Colorplate 19.
The bedcover of which this is a border detail was worked after a European pattern in India, probably in Bengal, for the Portuguese market. Indian, about 1600–1625. Height of border: 25.5 cm. (10 in.). Museum of Fine Arts, Boston, Elizabeth Day McCormick Collection, 1950

Kutch and Sind (colorplate 18) are particularly familiar; some of them show geometric designs executed in counted-thread work, others have curvilinear patterns requiring a drawing on the foundation to guide the needle or hook. There are bird and plant motifs, as well as animal and human figures, worked on colored cottons or silks with brightly colored silk yarns and occasionally applications of bits of mirrored glass. The small rumals (covers for offerings and gifts) from Chamba in the Himalayas (plate 82)—either embroidered or painted by the resist-dyeing process—depict energetic figures, animals and flowers derived from local styles of painting.

Like China, India produced a large body of needlework for export to the West. The chief markets were England and Portugal, two nations whose history became involved with India's in the sixteenth century. In Bengal in the seventeenth century great bedcovers and bed hangings made for the Portuguese market (plate 83) were worked on plain or dyed cotton or silk with yarns of yellow silk alone or silks of several colors and incorporated both native and European motifs. Typically the patterns were executed in chain stitches through two layers of fabric: a heavy support layer and a finer fabric on the front. All kinds of real and fanciful birds, beasts and humanoid figures appear along with flowers and heraldic patterns. One polychrome example, worked with colored silks on a foundation of dark blue silk, shows a battle scene in the field and flowers, figures and animals in the border (colorplate 19).

For export to the West, Indian needleworkers also produced the large textiles called palampores, which show the flowering tree often misnamed the Tree of Life. These trees are first cousins to the ones on English and American bed curtains and on curtains made in India for export to the West (plates 15–17 and 49–50, see pages 20–21 and 58); it has been suggested their origin is European, not Oriental.

Perhaps the most familiar of all nineteenth-century Indian textiles are the shawls woven in Kashmir and exported to Europe. Their vogue in Europe began at the end of the eighteenth century and lasted almost a hundred years. Early in the nineteenth century, shawl makers in India started to decorate similar warm, fine wool fabrics with needlework instead of constructing them by the slower and more expensive tapestry-weaving process originally used, and at first glance these embroidered shawls appear identical to the woven ones (plate 80).

Around 1830 a new kind of pattern developed that involved scenes from well-known Indo-Persian poems and stories; it was apparently made for the domestic Indian market. The purely ornamental pieces were made largely for export, and these shawls, like the shawls from China, changed size and shape as the silhouette of dresses changed in the West during the nineteenth century, growing from the size of stoles and shoulder wraps until they became large enough to drape around the body like a cloak.

5 Western Asia and the Near East

Among the diverse types of embroidery practiced within the borders of the Soviet Union the needlework from several parts of Üzbekistan (Üzbek Soviet Socialist Republic, formerly part of Turkestan) is probably the most striking. Many of the patterns worked in and around the city of Bukhara in this region derive from earlier Turkish ceramics, brocades and velvets from Asia Minor. The motifs are usually highly stylized flowers and leaves worked in colored silk yarns on plain-weave cotton foundations, but it is Bukhara stitch, a distinctive self-couching stitch, that gives these embroideries their characteristic effect: the pattern stands out boldly against the foundation in relatively high relief. Some of these pieces have been dated as early as the eighteenth century; the majority—like the vivid bed cover in colorplate 20—probably date from the nineteenth century, but covers in this style continued to be made into the early twentieth.

In northwest Persia and the Caucasus, needleworkers produced magnificent cushion covers and larger rectangular pieces that may have served as floor mats. The surviving pieces probably date from the seventeenth to nineteenth centuries. Some are patterned with small-scale geometric or stylized plant forms completely covering the surface; others have large hook, leaf and swirl forms reminiscent of the patterns of certain Caucasian knotted carpets (plate 84).

Embroiderers in urban centers in Persia were of course influenced by fashions emanating from the court, and they produced hangings, covers and costume fabrics that show the same sophisticated elegance that marks the great polychrome velvets and brocades the Persian weavers produced from the sixteenth to nineteenth centuries. As we have seen, this style also influenced the taste of the Mughal court, and it is often difficult today to distinguish the needlework of one court style from that of the other. However, there are a number of types of Persian embroidery from the later years that clearly proclaim their national origin. Among the most familiar are the pieces with small-

Colorplate 20.
Made in Turkestan, this bedcover is typical of so-called Bukhara work in its use of a white background as a foil for the sparkling colors of the silk embroidery yarns. Nineteenth century. Height: 243.5 cm. (96 in.). Museum of Fine Arts, Boston, gift of Mary E. Williams, 1945

scale floral ornaments arranged solidly over the surface in diagonal rows. Because of Victorian delicacy in referring to certain kinds of garments, these fabrics were called *gilets persans* (Persian waist-coats) in the West. They were in fact the material used for women's trousers in Persia—and the fabric was referred to there as *nakshe* (plate 85). It was worked in direct imitation of the more expensive silk and metal woven fabrics made for the same purpose. During this period also, the widely known applied-work prayer carpets or hang-ings of Resht were made (plate 86). They depicted a prayer niche (mihrab) containing a tree, flowers and birds, which was framed by several elaborate borders. Sometimes the pieces of colored wool were piled up in layers in the usual way to create the pattern; in other ex-amples pieces were cut out and fitted together like a mosaic, the edges covered by couched gilt cords. In both types details were added with chain stitches in silk.

The needleworkers of the Ottoman Empire have left a wealth of material representing the culture of Asia Minor (Asiatic Turkey), the heartland of the empire, as well as the cultures of Armenia, the Greek mainland and islands, the Balkans and the entire southern shore of the Mediterranean, for all these regions at one time or another formed part of the vast empire that endured from the late thirteenth century

84.
This large embroidered cushion cover or floor mat from the southern Caucasus shows many motifs similar to those in certain knotted carpets from the same area. Probably eighteenth century. Length: 164 cm. (64½ in.). Museum of Fine Arts, Boston, Elizabeth Day McCormick Col-lection, 1943

85.
Tent-stitched cotton fabric like this, showing diagonal bands of flowers em-broidered in colored silks, was used to make women's trousers in Persia. Eigh-teenth–nineteenth century. Length: 68 cm. (26¾ in.). Museum of Fine Arts, Boston, gift of Mrs. William F. Wharton, 1931

86.
Shaped pieces of wool joined in mosaic fashion form the elaborate flower and bird pattern of this prayer carpet or hanging from Resht. Persian, nineteenth century. Height: 190 cm. (75 in.). Metro-politan Museum of Art, New York, Rogers Fund, 1910

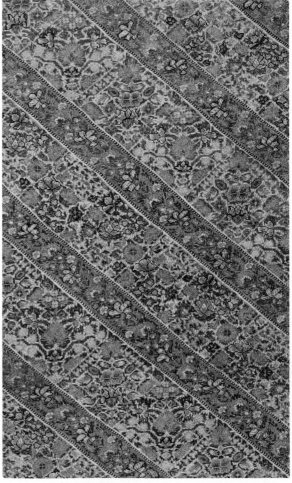

84

85

87.
The large-scale, brilliantly colored patterns embroidered on this section of a sumptuous hanging are based on earlier Turkish brocaded silks and velvets. Turkish, eighteenth century. Height: 221 cm. (87 in.). Museum of Fine Arts, Boston, Ross Collection, 1915

to the early twentieth. The grander Turkish pieces, most of which were embroidered by skillful housewives to decorate their own persons and homes, show bold, sumptuous patterns derived from Asia Minor's sixteenth- and seventeenth-century brocaded silks and velvets (plate 87).

We all use what we call Turkish towels every day, but like "Turkey work" the term is beset by confusion. From the eighteenth century onward European and American travelers brought home quite another kind of "Turkish towel." These were gorgeous strips of cloth, richly embroidered with bright silks and gleaming metal yarns, and many of them had bands of loop weaving that undoubtedly inspired someone to call terry cloth "Turkish toweling" when it appeared on the market. In their native lands, the "towels" were used as towels on special occasions like births, circumcisions and weddings, and as napkins at festive dinners, but they were prized also as scarves, kerchiefs, gift wrappings and headstone covers. There is an endless variety of patterns—flowers, buildings, boats, trees and landscapes— all worked in silks and silver and gilt yarns and tinsels, usually on plain- or twill-weave linen foundations (plate 88).

Among embroideries of the Ottoman Empire associated specifically with the culture of Armenia, the most familiar are the hangings or bedcovers made in Marash in Asia Minor (plate 89). These are worked in colored cotton yarns on plain-weave, often blue cotton foundations. Like other embroideries from Asia Minor, their patterns sound a distant echo of motifs on sixteenth- and seventeenth-century brocades and velvets. The Marash embroideries date from the eighteenth to the early twentieth century, but most are probably from the nineteenth.

On the Greek mainland and in the neighboring territories, including the Greek islands, local traditions diluted the taste of the Ottoman Empire enough to enable us to identify the specific regions where many of the embroideries of this area were worked. Festival costumes made in Greece and the Balkan countries to the north display a love of couched gilt cording and dense silk stitches. The Albanian woman's sleeveless coat in plate 90 is worked with opulent gilt cords and tapes. In similar coats long open sleeves permitted the sleeves of the garment beneath the coat to show through; these sleeves too were embroidered. In the Attica region and on some of the Greek islands women wore floor-length sleeveless tunics of heavy cotton that were embroidered around the hem with deep bands of rich ornament (colorplate 21). Even after the woman was fully dressed, the decorated hems remained in sight below the other parts of her costume.

Enchanting embroideries, mostly cushion covers, dating from the eighteenth and nineteenth centuries, were produced in the region of Epirus on the Ionian coast of northern Greece and possibly also on some of the islands off that coast (colorplate 26). These usually represent human figures (often horsemen or a bride with her groom

88

89

88.
Intended for both practical and ceremonial uses, this exceptionally fine ornamental towel characteristically has architectural and floral patterns in its embroidered ends. Turkish, eighteenth century. Length: 171 cm. (67⅜ in.). Detail. Museum of Fine Arts, Boston, bequest of Mrs. Arthur Croft, 1901

89.
The colorful tulip motifs satin-stitched on the blue foundation of this Armenian cotton bedcover from Marash in what is now Turkey illustrate the tradition among Near Eastern needleworkers of borrowing motifs from the costly woven brocades and velvets of earlier centuries. Armenian, nineteenth century. Height: 138 cm. (54¼ in.). Museum of Fine Arts, Boston, Ross Collection, 1923

COLORPLATE 21

COLORPLATE 22

Colorplate 21.
Constructed of tapered cotton strips on which colored silk yarns are worked in Gobelin and several other stitches, this border adorned the hem of a sleeveless tunic belonging to a woman from the Attica region of Greece. Nineteenth or early twentieth century. Height of border: 45.7 cm. (18 in.). Detail. Cooper-Hewitt Museum, gift of Mary H. Ward, 1931

Colorplate 22.
A frieze of flowers, mermaids and birds decorates this fragment of a Cretan woman's skirt. These particular ornaments are unique to Crete among the several Greek islands known for their needlework. Probably nineteenth century. Height: 29 cm. (11½ in.). Cooper-Hewitt Museum, gift of George Arnold Hearn, 1943

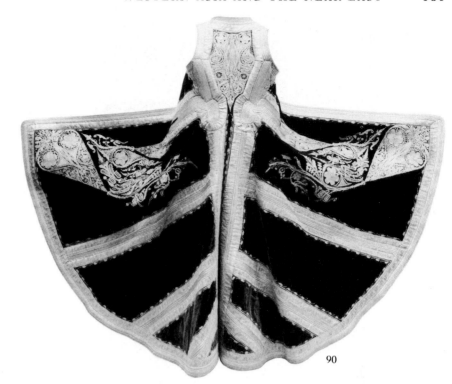

90

90.
The Albanian woman who wore this gilt-trimmed velvet sleeveless coat when dressed for festive occasions also wore a tunic, jacket or blouse, trousers, cap and jewelry to complete her elaborate ensemble. Albanian, late nineteenth or early twentieth century. Honolulu Academy of Arts, gift of Mrs. Ben Norris, 1964

91.
Meant to be hung from a large ring set in the ceiling above the bed, this red, green and white bed tent from Rhodes is a Greek island version of the grand bed draperies of Europe. Greek, eighteenth or early nineteenth century. Height: 358 cm. (141 in.). Metropolitan Museum of Art, New York, Rogers Fund, 1904

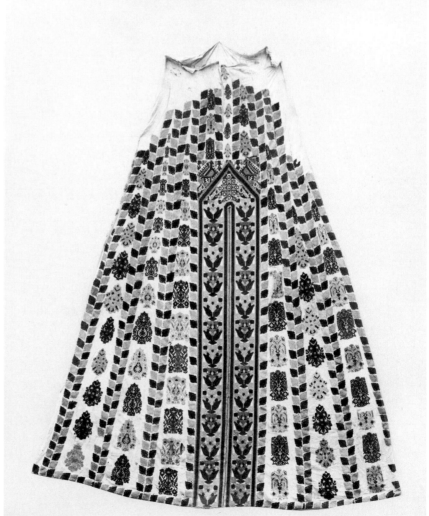

91

Colorplate 23.
Palestinian brides wore this version of the *djillayeh*, a kind of dress appearing in various forms throughout Palestine at the time of the British mandate, 1920–48. British Museum, London, 1968

Colorplate 24.
In this single motif from a handsome Chechaouèn cover for a cushion or roll of bedclothes, intricate geometric forms reflect the taste of both Moorish Spain and North Africa. Moroccan, nineteenth century. Length: 160 cm. (63 in.). Detail. Detroit Institute of Arts, gift of Francis Waring Robinson, 1946

92.
Ottoman taste influenced the pattern of this Algerian scarf or towel, but the choice of colors and the use of deflected-element embroidery are distinctly Algerian. Nineteenth century. Length: 355 cm. (140 in.). Detail. Museum of Fine Arts, Boston, bequest of Mrs. Arthur Croft, 1901

and parents) combined with enormous birds, flowers and inanimate objects that are joyfully out of scale.

In the Greek islands, each group of islands—in most cases, each island individually—developed specific local traditions of needlework that enable us to pinpoint almost all embroideries from the islands relatively easily. The island embroideries were made by women at home to decorate their simple houses with fabrics that shine with the colors and gloss of colored silks. Most of the surviving examples were made in the nineteenth century, a few perhaps in the eighteenth.

The magnificent embroidered bed tents from the Dodecanese Islands, particularly Rhodes, Kos and Patmos, are especially impressive (plate 91). These were made of strips of linen tapered at one end and sewn together to form a circular tent that was hung over the bed on a ring suspended from the ceiling. Each panel had the same pattern, except for the one in the center front, which had borders and a pediment for the "door"—simply a slit in the fabric that allowed access to the interior sleeping space.

On most of the Greek islands needleworkers made elaborate covers for the cushions which were stacked on the floor or on a dais and, along with the bed hangings, valances and other embroideries, provided the major decoration of the house. Needleworkers on Naxos in the Cyclades group and on Thasos in the northern Aegean made covers that depended for their special effect on some ingenious counted-thread patterns (colorplate 25 and see also plate 106, page 118). Both the Naxos and Thasos covers employ interesting techniques. The stitches are so perfectly placed and the foundation is so open in texture that one might at first mistake these embroideries for pieces of weaving. It is only the fact that the darning stitches are worked parallel to *both* the warp and weft directions (rather than just the weft direction, as one would expect in a simple structure like this) that gives one pause; an examination of the back of the fabric makes it evident that the textiles were patterned with needlework after the weaving was completed, rather than with a shuttle or bobbin during the weaving.

Crete's needleworkers have left us both a delightful group of embroideries and a special feather stitch that has been named after the island. It is not only this stitch that gives Cretan work its highly distinctive character but also the nature of its patterns, which are markedly different from those of the other islands. Stylized flowers arranged as though in vases, birds and double-tailed mermaids compose themselves into symmetrical units that repeat horizontally (colorplate 22). Although the taste of Asia Minor is here, the organization of the shapes relates more to the taste of sixteenth-century Italy. Indeed, there are echoes of earlier Italian needlework in the embroideries of most of the Greek islands, especially those counted-thread embroideries appearing now and then that are certainly sur-

Colorplate 23

Colorplate 24

vivals of the silk and linen borders worked from printed patterns in sixteenth- and seventeenth-century Italy and Spain.

The patterns of Palestinian needlework are totally different from those of the Greek mainland or islands or the Balkans, even though Palestine was also part of the Ottoman Empire until its dissolution in 1918. The wives of Arab farmers living in villages along the Mediterranean coast or in the neighboring hills produced the work, which has survived mostly in embroidered dresses, veils and trouser legs as well as cushion covers. The handsome *djillayeh* (dress) in colorplate 23 was made by needleworkers living in the highlands of southern Judea or on the plains of the southeast coast and dates from the period of the British mandate (1920–48). Like other Palestinian garments of the nineteenth and twentieth centuries, this example has needlework on the chest and back panels and on the skirt. The character and arrangement of the needlework, as well as the very wide wing sleeves, indicate that this *djillayeh* was a wedding dress.

The taste of Asia Minor also influenced the style of needlework produced in North Africa, an area that remained almost in its entirety within the Ottoman Empire until 1918, but women in Tunisia, Algeria and Morocco worked many kinds of fabrics in their own regional styles. The pattern, color and gleaming surface of the Algerian scarf or towel shown in plate 92, for instance, recall Asia Minor work in a general way, but the color scheme of blue, violet and red, with touches of pink, green and black, is particularly and specifically Algerian. Scarves or towels and veils were used primarily as headdresses. Similar work, using mainly couched, brick and deflected-element embroidery stitches on a fine plain-weave linen fabric with relatively open mesh, was applied to long, narrow rectangular lengths of linen that were subsequently joined side by side with strips of striped silk ribbon to make curtains.

Moroccan work shows more variation than Algerian. Each of the major needlework centers—Azemmour, Fez, Meknès, Rabat, Salé, Chechaouèn and Tétouan (Tetuán)—had a pronounced local style. Because of Morocco's close cultural contacts with Spain from the eighth century on, its needlework was more influenced by European styles than was the needlework of any other of the North African cultures. Most of the patterns used in Moroccan cities have highly stylized floral patterns rendered chiefly in cross stitch. Silk embroideries made in Tétouan used sleek, polychrome floral patterns that were much more naturalistic than the others. In contrast, the needlework of Chechaouèn (colorplate 24) showed a dependence on complex geometric shapes, especially interlaced knots and stars, that might be regarded not only as a reflection of the formal vocabulary of Moorish Spain but also as a survival of earlier Arabic ornaments developed in North Africa itself, the source of much Moorish ornament in Spain.

Colorplate 25.
The striking chevron pattern of this cushion cover from the Greek island of Thasos was worked with silk yarns in darning stitches by counting the threads of a cotton ground. Probably nineteenth century. Length: 104 cm. (41 in.). Detail. Cooper-Hewitt Museum, gift of the Provident Securities Company, 1955

Colorplate 26.
The entertaining out-of-scale motifs on this cushion cover from the Epirus district of northwestern Greece were a specialty of embroiderers in that area. Probably eighteenth century. Height: 43.2 cm. (17 in.). Museum of Fine Arts, Boston, Elizabeth Day McCormick Collection, 1943

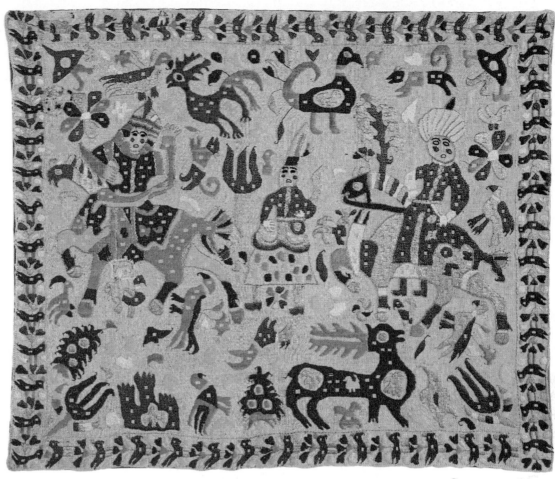

COLORPLATE 26

COLORPLATE 25

6 Needlework of the Indigenous Peoples of Africa and America

For some reason—we do not yet know what it is—the indigenous peoples of Africa and America did not develop the art of needlework with the same diversity that we have seen elsewhere in the world. Needlework among these peoples almost always reflected images created in such other techniques as basket weaving, carving and pottery making, or such special techniques as bark inlaying and sand painting. The blanket in plate 97, for example, looks as though its pattern came straight from a totem pole. The only notable exception is the needlework of pre-Conquest Peru (before A.D. 1532), which constitutes an art form of astonishingly high development with a wealth of imagery that is as rich as any produced elsewhere.

Most indigenous African embroideries display entirely local patterns. Among the most familiar are the pile raffia cloths made by the Kuba people of the Republic of Zaire, in central Africa (plate 93). Fibers from the raffia palm tree that the Kuba cultivate in the Kasai River region formed the substance of the yarns that were used both for weaving the mat foundation and for the embroidery itself. The needleworked patterns were given names and special meanings, and were worn as a sign of high rank.

In regions where people adopted the religion of Islam, needlework shows the influence of Arabic culture. The Nigerian robe in plate 96 represents a typical West African outer garment for a man. The wide, loose robe is worn over trousers. Needlework decorates a panel of fabric applied over the chest, and patterns are also worked on the garment itself next to the applied panel. Since strict Islamic doctrine, which these Nigerian people follow, rules out representation of living creatures, the patterns here are geometric or fanciful—swirling spirals, interlaced knots, toothed shapes and the like. Professional male embroiderers produce these and other kinds of needlework in this region. A closely related repertoire of patterns appears on the trousers of men living in the region that includes northwest Nigeria, southern Niger

Colorplate 27.
Monkeylike figures combined with snakes, fish and trophy heads appear on this ancient embroidered mantle, which was preserved for centuries among the wrappings of a mummy. Peruvian, late Paracas culture, 300–100 B.C. Height of entire mantle: 90 cm. (35½ in.). Detail. Museum of Fine Arts, Boston, Ross Collection, 1916

93

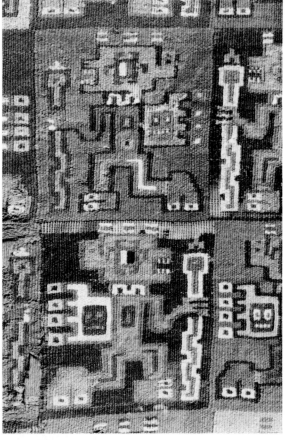

94

and Upper Volta. Again, the cut and ornamentation of these garments show direct influence from the cultures of Islam. The pair of ceremonial trousers in colorplate 29 (see page 114) were made for a chief of the Mossi people living in the region of Ouagadougou, Upper Volta.

Other indigenous African peoples—those who did not embrace the stricter forms of the Muslim religion—did not operate under the constraint forbidding the depiction of living creatures. In Dahomey (now the People's Republic of Benin), for example, male needleworkers among the Fon people made pictorial wall hangings by means of applied work using colorful cotton fabrics. This tradition seems to have traveled to America with the slave trade and bloomed again in the southern United States (plate 69, see page 76).

The history of needlework among indigenous people in the Western Hemisphere can be traced much further back in time. Through the chance circumstances of climate and burial customs, we have embroideries from indigenous American cultures that predate those from every other culture except that of ancient Egypt, and they have survived for the same reasons. The coast of Peru, particularly in the south, is dry, and its natives habitually mummified their dead and buried them with grave furnishings, including sets of garments. Most of these garments were woven, but the oldest we have happen to show embroidered rather than woven patterns. They date from the period of the Paracas culture, which flourished in the south coastal region for more than a thousand years, beginning about 1400 B.C. The most familiar fabrics from these burials appear in the mantles, the ponchos, and the skirt and turban cloths worked in stem or darning stitches with colored wool yarns on plain-weave wool foundations (plate 95). The yarns were spun from the hair of the native cameloid animals, especially the alpaca and vicuña. The patterns depict animal and human shapes as well as birds and what appear to be fanciful figures incorporating parts of different kinds of creatures (colorplate 27). Many Paracas embroideries have border motifs worked in three dimensions like tabs; it is believed that these were worked with a single needle rather than a pair of knitting needles, using knit-stem and buttonhole stitches. The stitches on the body of the garment lie flat against the foundation fabric in the normal way and often cover it entirely. Embroideries from later periods of pre-Conquest Peruvian culture have survived in some numbers. Certain of these proclaim their needlework nature clearly, like the pieces worked with chain stitches. Others were patterned so perfectly with darning or running stitches that it is almost impossible to distinguish them from products of the loom (plate 94).

At the northern end of the Pacific coastline that links the North and South American continents, decorative needlework is seen on the

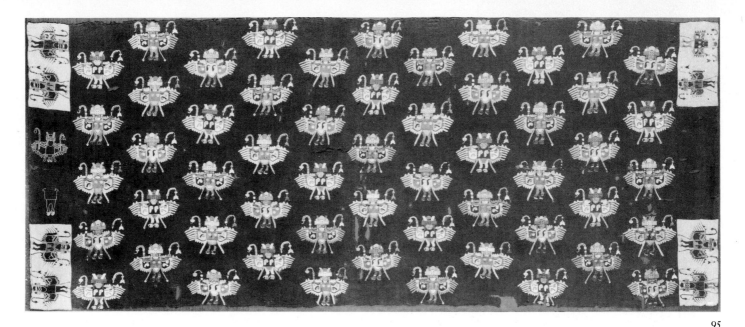

93.
Raffia yarns in stem and looped stitches, on a plain-weave raffia foundation, are cut to form a pile-surfaced dress fabric, with handsome lozenge and chevron designs. African, Zaire, Kuba people, probably twentieth century. Length: 74.3 cm. (29¼ in.). Cooper-Hewitt Museum, gift of Mrs. Charles F. Morgan, 1951

94.
Ancient Peruvian embroiderers worked with extraordinary precision, and this highly refined needleworked fabric, a fragment of a garment or hanging, could easily be mistaken for a woven piece. Peruvian, Huari culture, about 500–1200. Height: 49.5 cm. (19½ in.). Metropolitan Museum of Art, New York, gift of George D. Pratt, 1930

95.
Because it was buried for 2000 years under ideal conditions, this ancient wool mantle, stem-stitched with anthropomorphic figures, still shows vividly colored yarns and patterns. Peruvian, late Paracas culture, 300–100 B.C. Height: 120.5 cm. (47½ in.). Museum of Fine Arts, Boston, Ross Collection, 1916

96.
Trousers were worn under this man's robe from West Africa. The chest panel has been applied, and further stitching is worked alongside. African, Nigeria, Hausa people, about 1945. American Museum of Natural History, New York, bought by Mrs. Menedes MacKay in 1948

outer suits worked by Eskimo women. Throughout the Arctic area people embroidered both sealskins and fishskins with yarns of moose and caribou hair and made warm, waterproof garments. To the south, in southeastern Alaska and coastal British Columbia, the Haida, Kwakiutl and Tlingit people embroidered ceremonial shirts and blankets with various nontextile materials, including small shells, buttons, coins, beads and abalone shell. Surviving pieces, which date from the nineteenth or early twentieth century, usually use as their foundations wool fabrics that came into the region as articles of trade. The handsome button blankets made by the Tlingit people, for example, often have blankets from the Hudson's Bay Company as their foundation fabrics (plate 97).

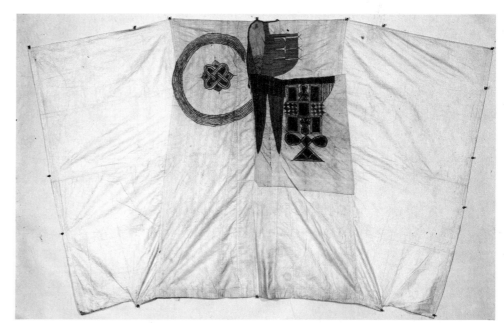

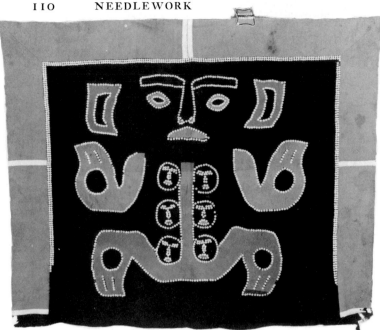

97

98

97.
Some needleworkers in western Canada and Alaska used mother-of-pearl buttons to make their work glisten. Applications of napped red wool as well as buttons decorate the napped black wool foundation of this ceremonial blanket, which is bordered with strips of red wool. Alaskan, Tlingit people, late nineteenth or early twentieth century. Height: 139.7 cm. (55 in.). Detroit Institute of Arts, Octavia W. Bates Fund, 1977

98.
The Mexican needleworker who embroidered this cotton furniture cover made the most of the expensive silk yarns used by employing stitches, including couched work, that placed most of the yarn on the front of the fabric and very little on the back. Mexican, probably eighteenth century. Width: 61 cm. (24 in.). Detail. San Antonio Museum Association (Witte Memorial Museum), gift of Miss Florence Jaggi and Mrs. Pearl Lentz, 1956

Still farther south, in the region that is now the continental United States, the indigenous people in almost every section practiced some form of needlework—particularly beadwork and quill embroidery on leather or bark foundations. This subject is complex, but fortunately it has been well studied, and anyone interested in pursuing it can find authoritative texts. We have room here for only the few general observations that follow.

In the southwest, the leading practitioners of ornamental stitchery were the peoples of the Pueblo culture, who decorated men's shirts and women's dresses with back, darning, satin, chain and buttonhole stitches. The patterns on Pueblo clothing show a family resemblance to those on Pueblo baskets.

During the nineteenth century and later, the hunters of the plains, Great Lakes and Mississippi Valley practiced a second type of needlework, which involved using European silk ribbons to make applied-work ornaments for skirts, moccasins, mantles and trouser legs (plate 99).

The third major category of North American Indian needlework was developed by the Seminole people in the Everglades region of Florida. This was a patchwork technique utilizing brightly colored cotton fabrics in which small, angular bits of cotton were worked into textiles for men's shirts and trousers and women's blouses and skirt bands.

In Latin America indigenous motifs—including certain geometric shapes that formed themselves naturally and easily on the loom—were worked side by side with patterns derived from European needlework. The resulting interrelation of woven and needleworked fabrics is so intimate that one kind of fabric is often mistaken for the other.

Mexican needleworkers produced a rich and varied body of embroideries that show patterns developed in a number of Mexico's regional cultures; many of these pieces have survived. There are also large numbers of embroidered samplers, as well as embroidered furnishing and costume fabrics that testify to the extension of pure Spanish culture into the Western Hemisphere. Furniture covers worked in Mexico by the descendants of European immigrants, or by native people working in the European tradition, from the sixteenth century onward show the familiar floral, bird, human and animal shapes that served as patterns for contemporary embroiderers in Spain and Portugal (plate 98). The national costumes of Mexico—the *china poblana* for women, the *charro* for men—are also lavishly embroidered in the European tradition. The former is based on a European concept of Chinese needlework of the Ch'ing dynasty; the second derives from the embroidery on European men's costumes of the baroque period. Floral patterns of the European type also found favor in the villages of Mexico, where they were used to decorate fiesta costumes like the long shirts worn by Zapotec girls in the state of Oaxaca (plate 100).

The various regions and villages of Guatemala also produced handsome needleworked fabrics. Women's sleeveless shirts were enriched with both woven and embroidered decorations (here, too, the techniques are often difficult to distinguish). The shirts made in the region of Chichicastenango have a typical look that depends in part on a technique combining applied work and stitches with woven ornamentation (plate 101).

Probably the most distinctive needlework of all the indigenous Central American cultures is that practiced by the Cuna Indian women of the islands bordering the San Blas Gulf off the Caribbean coast of Panama. Their special version of applied work seems to have developed soon after 1850, with the island women first using it to make chemises for themselves. Around 1900 the shape of the costume changed: the chemise shortened into a blouse, and a piece of printed trade cotton was wrapped around the lower body as a skirt. The blouse continued to be made by the characteristic applied-work technique, mostly reverse applied work. Two rectangular panels of this applied work (the *molas*) form the front and back of the blouse; at the top they are sewn to a shallow shoulder piece that has small puffed sleeves. The resulting garment falls loose at the waist (colorplate 28).

99.
Silk ribbons, imported from Europe, reached the Indians of the north central United States sometime in the nineteenth century and were used to make applied-work ornaments like these bands for a woman's leggings. American, Potawatomi people, late nineteenth or early twentieth century. American Museum of Natural History, New York, acquired by Alanson Skinner in 1912

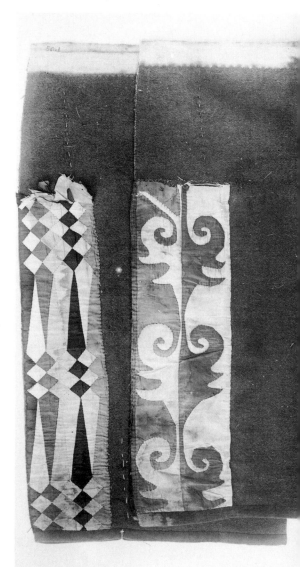

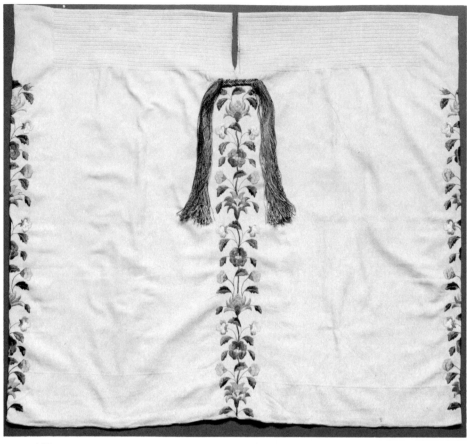

100

Bird motifs on the chest and back panels (*molas*) of this woman's blouse are rendered in the standard and reverse applied work perfected by the Cuna Indian women. Panamanian, about 1900–1925. Cooper-Hewitt Museum, gift of Mrs. John Winslow, 1960

100.
For festivals Zapotec girls of Yalalag in the state of Oaxaca wore long sleeveless cotton shirts like this one embroidered with multicolored flowers in glossy silks worked mainly in satin stitches. Mexican, probably early twentieth century. Metropolitan Museum of Art, New York, Costume Institute, gift of Irene Lewisohn, 1939

101.
Inlaid silk weaving was combined with needlework to create the dazzling ornaments decorating this sleeveless cotton shirt for a woman of Chichicastenango. Guatemalan, late nineteenth or early twentieth century. Metropolitan Museum of Art, New York, gift of Joseph Downs, 1946

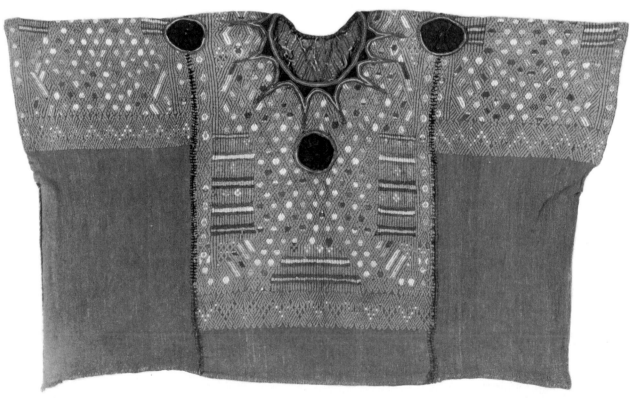

101

7 About Studying and Collecting Needlework

To make the best of their resources, beginning collectors will want to develop a sense of attribution and quality before going into the marketplace. The experienced collector never stops reading, never misses a chance to look at and feel objects. Indeed, continued study is one of the keenest pleasures the collector knows, and it becomes a creative force in life. It is the collectors—private people, dealers, museum curators, needleworkers looking for inspiration in the past—who make the discoveries, publish the new facts and experience the incomparable joy of sharing knowledge with their fellows.

Collectors collect information as well as objects, and a collector's most prized possession is a pair of discriminating eyes. These he cannot buy; he must acquire them through long practice, exercising both the intellect and the senses, especially sight and touch. Reading may come first, and it is essential, for it is a way of building the framework on which one will eventually hang the new facts and images drawn from looking at pieces of needlework and, whenever possible, studying them in the hand, getting to know the feel of certain fabrics and yarns. No book can teach these lessons, of course, nor is it expected to.

Because textile dyes are notoriously subject to fading, and fibers to deterioration, through long exposure to light, examples of old needlework may not appear in museum galleries in large numbers at any one time. It is in fact necessary to seek them out in the storerooms and study rooms, with the help and cooperation of the staff. Fortunately for the student of needlework, most large art museums and some natural history museums maintain staff specialists who, given sufficient notice, will make examples of needlework available to the serious researcher for study. This sort of physical contact with needlework is invaluable for both beginning and advanced collectors, but it is necessarily limited and limiting: the rules for handling old embroideries in public collections are naturally strict.

Colorplate 29.
These ceremonial trousers for an African chieftain show typical stylized patterns found in the needlework of West Africa. African, Upper Volta, Mossi people, late nineteenth or early twentieth century. Metropolitan Museum of Art, New York, Irene Lewisohn Bequest Fund, 1971

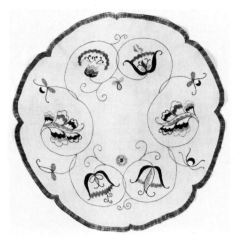

102.
In this modern doily from the Society of
Blue and White Needlework, the needleworker has imitated eighteenth-century prototypes like the one in plate 103. American,
about 1900. Diameter: 59.3 cm. (23⅜ in.).
Museum of Fine Arts, Boston, bought by
special contribution, 1945

103.
Two shades of blue crewel yarn are used in
this authentic eighteenth-century New England piece—part of a bedcover. American,
1750–75. Height: 122 cm. (48 in.). Museum
of Fine Arts, Boston, gift of Mrs. Henrietta
Page, 1926

Still and all, despite the special opportunities museums offer collectors to see and touch rare and beautiful old needlework, sooner
or later the collector will have to buy examples that may be handled
at will in order to see how they were made and with what materials.

There are dealers who specialize in textiles, including antique embroideries; but these are the exception and they exist in only a few
great cities. Most collectors buy examples of needlework at antique
shops or fairs that offer other kinds of objects as well. Occasionally—
but only very occasionally—a collector may find a desirable acquisition
in a private home where family possessions have been kept in place
for generations.

The other major source of material is the auction house. Examples
of old needlework, especially samplers, hangings and covers of various
sorts, and ecclesiastical vestments, turn up in general sales; sometimes
special auction sales also feature (or are limited to) furnishing fabrics
and costumes from the past, many or most of which have needleworked decorations.

The beginning collector may find it advisable to begin by buying
small, relatively simple pieces like needleworked pictures and samplers
—especially samplers, which are usually dated, often show the name
of the maker and the place she lived, and by their very nature are easy
to analyze in terms of stitchery. Except for the important pieces,
which are either fully documented or particularly handsome, samplers
are also relatively inexpensive.

The entire question of price in the field of historical needlework is a
difficult one. There is so much less material available than there is, say,
in the field of furniture or glass, and the number of collectors is so
much smaller, that the market in old needlework is not so clearly
defined in terms of price as the market in most other kinds of
antiques. The most any collector can hope to do is to learn what prices
embroideries of different kinds and qualities have brought in recent
years and go on from there as best he can to develop a sense of price
in the field.

When it comes to the question of honest copies and outright
forgeries that may find their way into the market, there is not much
the collector can do but develop a sense of authenticity and whenever
possible seek the guidance of an impartial specialist. Nevertheless, we
can offer a few words of advice about three areas that may cause
concern: survivals, revivals and imitations.

Because decorating textiles by hand with a needle requires no
machines or major capital investment, embroiderers in the past were
more at liberty than weavers to repeat, revive or continue styles and
fashions of earlier periods—whatever the intention might be. Sometimes the conservative requirements of church patronage caused very
early styles to survive to modern times, as happened in the Greek
and Russian Orthodox churches. The choice of subjects, Byzantine

style of drawing, materials and workmanship in any Orthodox vestment were so firmly fixed by tradition that today we have difficulty separating sixteenth-century from nineteenth-century examples.

In other cases a deliberate though innocent wish to imitate earlier styles of needlework gave rise to a group of embroideries that look superficially so much like the originals that one may easily mistake one for the other. Much of the crewel work executed by amateur needleworkers during the past twenty-five years in England and America was based so closely on eighteenth-century models from the same cultures that it takes very close scrutiny of the materials, drawing and colors to distinguish the new from the old work.

The embroideries made from 1896 to 1926 by the Society of Blue and White Needlework in Deerfield, Massachusetts, present the same problem. The founders, Margaret Whiting and Ellen Miller, both had training in art, and they set about copying or tracing patterns of eighteenth-century New England embroideries that were then put on modern foundation fabrics to be worked with modern materials by local women in a cottage industry. At first the embroideries had only blue and white patterns, but later more colors were added. They were worked with linen yarns on linen foundations, like some New England embroideries of the second half of the eighteenth century, and the Society used natural dyes. Even though under close examination the Deerfield materials may look different from the earlier ones, any apparent difference is probably not in itself a dependable criterion for judgments because one finds a wide variety of textures in true eighteenth-century embroideries. The Society marked its pieces with a capital letter *D* set as the hub of a spinning wheel; this helps identify the source, providing it is still present on the work. Comparing the Deerfield doily of plate 102 with the blue and white New England embroidery made in the third quarter of the eighteenth century of plate 103, one sees on one hand how closely the Society imitated these models, but on the other how different the character of the drawing and workmanship really is.

Revivals of historical styles in needlework were not limited to industrial enterprises like the Deerfield society. Any amateur embroiderer could imitate needlework from earlier periods within the limits of his or her ability. During the nineteenth century, for instance, when the imitating of earlier styles of furniture and clothing assumed the proportions of a style in itself, girls made copies of seventeenth-century raised-work pictures, as seen in plate 104. Looking at this picture by itself, one could easily mistake it for a true example of the type of seventeenth-century raised work now called stump work. Even when comparing it to an early example of stump work (plate 48, see page 57), one would probably not question the nineteenth-century piece because its clumsy appearance could easily be explained by assuming that the girl who worked it had less skill than the girl

104.
Imitating seventeenth-century English stump work (see plate 48), this raised-work picture was rendered with the traditional metal and colored silk yarns on a satin-weave foundation. American, about 1855–60. Height: 39.3 cm. (15½ in.). Chester County Historical Society, Chester, Penna.

105.
Although this Moroccan border was worked centuries after its Italian and Spanish prototypes were fashionable (see plate 44), it might be mistaken for one of the early pieces. Eighteenth or nineteenth century. Height: 25.5 cm. (10 in.). Metropolitan Museum of Art, New York, Rogers Fund, 1909

106.
The fact that the stitches can be mistaken for
extra warp or weft yarns makes it easy to
confuse the embroidered fabric of this nineteenth-century cushion cover from the
Greek island of Naxos with the similar
woven fabric shown in plate 107. Length:
114.3 cm. (45 in.). Detail. Honolulu Academy
of Arts, gift of Henrietta Brewer, 1933

107.
This twentieth-century power-woven fabric
imitates not only the pattern but the technique of the hand-embroidered cushion cover
in plate 106. Manufacturer not known.
Length (format almost square): 37.7 cm.
(12½ in.). Honolulu Academy of Arts, gift
of Henrietta Brewer, 1933

who worked the other. Such analyses require that one concentrate
on the dating of materials and details of workmanship.

The tradition of what is now called Assisi work in Italy, the silk-on-
linen border embroideries made by domestic needleworkers during the
Renaissance and later (plate 44, see page 48), was continued in the
Mediterranean area well into the twentieth century. Needleworkers
on some of the Greek islands and at Azemmour in Morocco produced
this work, as did embroiderers in Italy. The late Moroccan example in
plate 105 clearly demonstrates the survival of the Renaissance design
concept and of the technical procedure.

The last class of imitations to be considered here is that of woven
copies of earlier needleworked fabrics. Some embroideries can be
imitated almost exactly on the loom, particularly those that use pattern
darning or counted-thread work. A glance at the embroidered nineteenth-century Naxos cushion cover in plate 106, for instance, dis-
closes that it superficially resembles the twentieth-century woven
imitation in plate 107, but a closer look shows among other things that
the yarns in the embroidery create an effect of higher relief than the
woven yarns do.

Finally, the problem of repairs, restorations and alterations must be
considered. Many examples of early needlework have been treated to
restore damaged yarns and fabrics to what the restorer believed was
their original condition. If the restorer was sensitive and skillful and
used materials that might have been used originally, the most experienced eye might not be able to distinguish the restorations from the
original work, and it is important, especially for beginners, to know
this. It is equally important to learn to recognize later alterations in
the shape or construction of embroidered furnishing fabrics and garments. In these cases, as in simpler restorations, it is helpful, often
even essential, to compare the piece in question with a similar example
that is known to have survived intact.

Technical Notes

Incorporated here is information not included elsewhere about the materials and techniques used in making the needle-worked objects illustrated in the plates and colorplates. For items not listed, the relevant information will be found in the captions or text.

Frontispiece. Wall hanging. Linen canvas worked with colored silk and wool yarns in tent stitches and with couched gilt yarns.

Colorplate 1. Sampler. Plain-weave linen foundation worked with colored silk yarns in cross, satin, stem, chain, eyelet, couching, sheaf and speckling stitches.

Colorplate 4. Syon Cope. Plain-weave linen foundation worked with colored silk, gilt and silver yarns in underside couching, split stitch and laid and couched work.

Colorplate 6. Table carpet. Linen canvas worked with colored silk and silver yarns in split, tent, satin, brick and couching stitches.

Colorplate 7. Small purse. Front and back: plain-weave silk foundation worked with colored silk yarns in stem and long and short stitches, knots and couched silver and gilt yarns, purl, tinsel and spangles. Side pieces are made of green and silver woven fabric.

Colorplate 8. Firescreen panel. Canvas foundation with warp and wefts of cotton wrapped with silk (canvas intended for Berlin work) worked by counting threads, with colored wool yarns in cross stitches and loop stitches cut into a sculptured pile.

Colorplate 9. *King David and the Hanging of Absalom.* Satin-weave silk foundation worked with colored silk yarns in stem, satin and Romanian stitches, and with couched silver and gilt yarns and tinsel. The faces are painted on paper; the animals' eyes are made of beads.

Colorplate 10. Memorial picture. Painted plain-weave silk foundation worked with colored silk yarns mainly in long and short and stem stitches and with green and yellow chenille yarns (for the leaves, shrubs and plants) in a form of long and short or couched stitches.

Colorplate 12. Evening bag. Black silk velvet foundation worked with individual clear and opaque glass beads and with beaded sections worked separately on fine canvas and then applied to the velvet.

Colorplate 13. Crazy quilt. Pieced work, using plain-weave, pattern-woven and velvet silk fabrics joined with a variety of fancy stitches; backed with a satin fabric quilted by machine.

Colorplate 14. Rank badge. Satin-weave silk foundation worked with silk yarns in knotted stitches and with couched gilt yarns.

Colorplate 15. Taoist priest's robe. Satin-weave black silk foundation worked with colored silk yarns mainly in satin and double running stitches, couched gilt yarns of several weights and colors (greenish to reddish), and with colored silks laid over bits of gilt foil or paper.

Colorplate 16. Costume for the kabuki theater. Plain- and satin-weave silk foundations pieced and worked with colored silk and gilt yarns, mainly couched.

Colorplate 17. Woman's coat. Napped wool foundation with applied satin-weave silk; worked with colored silk yarns in satin, knotted, back and laid stitches and with couched gilt yarns and figured silk tape.

Colorplate 18. Head shawl. Plain-weave cotton foundation worked with colored silk yarns in chain, running, stem and buttonhole stitches.

Colorplate 19. Bedcover border detail. Satin-weave silk foundation worked with colored silks in chain stitches.

Colorplate 20. Bedcover. Plain-weave cotton foundation worked with colored silk yarns in Bukhara stitches.

Colorplate 22. Fragment of a woman's skirt. Plain-weave linen(?) foundation worked with colored silks in Cretan, fishbone, satin, stem, chain, long and short and knotted stitches.

Colorplate 23. *Djillayeh.* Plain-weave cotton foundation worked with applied pieces of cotton and with colored silk yarns mainly in cross stitches.

Colorplate 24. Cover. Plain-weave linen foundation worked with colored silks mainly in tent and plaited stitches.

Colorplate 26. Cushion cover. Plain-weave linen foundation worked with colored silk yarns in darning, herring-bone, chain and satin stitches.

Colorplate 27. Mantle. Plain-weave wool foundation worked with colored wool yarns in stem stitches.

Colorplate 28. Woman's blouse. Plain-weave cotton foundation worked with plain and printed cottons in applied work, both standard and reversed.

Colorplate 29. Ceremonial trousers. Plain-weave cotton foundation worked with colored silks mainly in chain and laid stitches.

PLATES

3. Curtain for a Torah ark. Satin-weave silk foundation worked with couched silver and gilt yarns and colored silk yarns.

4. Sampler. Plain-weave linen foundation worked with colored silk yarns in cross, satin, eyelet, chain, back, stem, Romanian and couching stitches.

5. Sampler. Plain-weave linen foundation worked with colored silk yarns in cross stitch.

6. Table cover border detail. Plain-weave linen foundation worked in double running stitches.

9. Cushion cover. Plain-weave linen foundation worked mainly in running and cross stitches.

11. Valance. Linen canvas worked with colored silk and wool yarns in tent stitches with touches of satin stitch.

13. Completed Berlin-work picture: *Familien Glück.* Canvas foundation worked with wool and silk yarns in tent and cross stitches of varying sizes.

15. Bed curtain. Plain-weave cotton, painted by the resist-dyeing process.

17. Fragment of a bed curtain (bottom section). Twill-weave foundation with linen warp and cotton wefts, worked with colored crewels in a wide range of flat, couched and knotted stitches.

21. Roundel. Plain-weave linen foundation worked with colored silk yarns in split, long and short, cross and couched stitches; applied to a piece of plain linen.

23. Length of embroidered dress fabric. Plain-weave silk foundation (with a brick

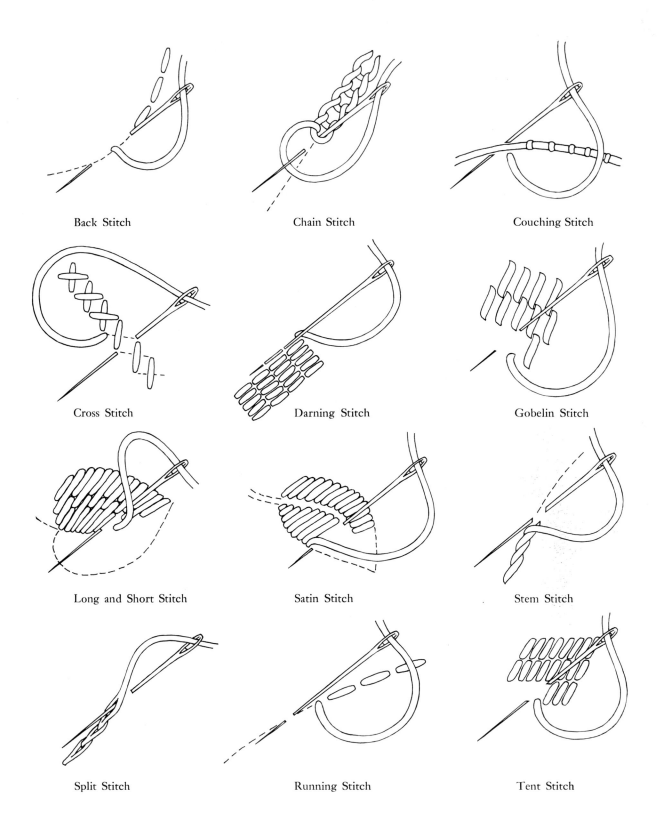

Back Stitch

Chain Stitch

Couching Stitch

Cross Stitch

Darning Stitch

Gobelin Stitch

Long and Short Stitch

Satin Stitch

Stem Stitch

Split Stitch

Running Stitch

Tent Stitch

pattern created by supplementary warp yarns) worked with colored silk yarns in long and short, satin and stem stitches.

25. Man's waistcoat. Worked with colored silk yarns in chain, stem, satin and bullion stitches; paste buttons.

26. Man's waistcoat. Worked with colored silk yarns in chain stitch with a hook.

28. Crewel rose. Twill-weave foundation fabric with linen warp and cotton wefts, worked with colored crewels.

31. *The Sacrifice of Isaac.* Worked with colored silk yarns mainly in tent and rococo stitches.

33. Box or book cover. Foundation fabric completely covered by needlework: the pictorial areas worked with long and short, satin and running stitches; the rest covered with couched fancy yarns of silk, metal or both, with raised motifs worked over padding or carved wood, and with beads.

35. Coverlet. Worked with applied plain and printed cottons and with colored silk yarns in chain, stem, buttonhole and knotted stitches.

36. Fragment of Hellenistic-style needlework. Twill-weave wool foundation worked in stem and chain stitches.

37. Hanging. Worked with colored wool yarns in chain and stem stitches.

38. Bayeux Tapestry. Plain-weave linen foundation worked with colored wool yarns in split, chain, laid and couched stitches.

42. *The Birth of the Virgin.* Plain-weave linen foundation worked with colored silk and gilt yarns in split, chain, stem and couching stitches and *or nué* technique.

44. Border of a furnishing fabric. Plain-weave linen foundation worked with red silk in long-arm cross and running stitches.

45. Wall panel. Satin-weave silk foundation worked in chain stitches, probably with a hook.

46. Wall panel. Satin-weave silk foundation worked with applied pieces of ribbed silk and painted satin and with colored silk yarns and silver yarns in chain and satin stitches.

47. Table carpet. Canvas foundation worked with colored silk yarns in tent stitches.

49. Bed hangings. Twill-weave foundation fabric with linen warp and cotton wefts, worked with colored crewels in stem, long and short, satin, chain, knotted and laid and couched stitches. The fabric of the valance was assembled recently from a number of pieces that were acquired separately but from the same source; the fringe is modern.

50. Bed hangings. Twill-weave foundation fabric with linen warp and cotton wefts, worked with colored crewels mainly in self-couching and flat stitches.

51. Floor carpet. Canvas foundation worked with colored wool yarns in cross and tent stitches.

52. Chair-seat cover. Twill-weave foundation fabric with linen warp and cotton wefts, worked with colored crewels mainly in self-couching and flat stitches.

54. Embroidered petticoat band. Plain-weave linen foundation worked with colored crewels mainly in self-couching, stem and knotted stitches.

55. Bed curtain. Plain-weave linen foundation worked with colored crewels mainly in stem, satin, chain and self-couching stitches.

56. Chimneypiece (frame shaped to hang over a mantel). Canvas worked with silk and wool yarns in tent stitches with some details in raised and knotted stitches and some metal yarns and beads.

57. Man's cap. Plain-weave linen foundation worked with yellow and blue silk yarns in satin, stem, fishbone, bullion and buttonhole stitches.

58. Pocketbook. Canvas worked with colored crewels in the flame pattern. The same kind of pattern also decorated many other sorts of needleworked fabrics in colonial America, including upholstery material for seat furniture, firescreens, book covers and women's inside pockets.

59. Fruit and bird picture. Satin-weave silk foundation worked with colored silk yarns mainly in long and short stitches.

60. Bed rug. Plain-weave wool foundation worked with looped running stitches; some loops cut.

61. Sampler. Plain-weave wool foundation worked with colored silk yarns in satin, stem and cross stitches and with couched chenille yarns.

62. *Warwick Castle.* Plain-weave silk foundation painted with gray washes and worked with black silk yarns in running, long and short and seed stitches.

65. Center section of a table cover. Plain-weave cotton foundation worked with cotton yarns mainly in withdrawn-element work and various relief and flat stitches; border of mixed bobbin and needlepoint lace (*point d'Angleterre*).

66. Hanging. Canvas worked with silk yarns in Gobelin and satin stitches.

71. Man's festival suit. Plain-weave wool foundation, napped, worked with colored wool yarns and braid.

72. Sleeve from a woman's blouse. Plain-weave linen foundation worked with black wool yarns mainly in stem, satin and Romanian stitches.

74. Towel end. Plain-weave linen foundation worked with white cotton yarns mainly in chain, satin and buttonhole stitches and passages of openwork showing several kinds of filling stitches.

76. Scarf or long cover. Plain-weave foundation worked in stem, buttonhole and satin stitches and openwork.

77. Shawl. Plain-weave black silk foundation worked with colored silk yarns in satin and long and short stitches. The embroidery is reversible, but the shawl is not finished on both sides.

78. Piece of kimono fabric. Damask-weave silk foundation worked with colored silk yarns mainly in satin and stem stitches and with couched gilt yarns.

79. Hanging. Plain-weave silk foundation worked with colored silk yarns in split, satin and couched stitches and with couched silver and gilt yarns.

80. Shawl. Twill-weave red wool foundation, pieced with a similar black fabric in the center, and worked with stem, satin and darning stitches; pieced multi-color border.

81. Cover. Plain-weave cotton foundation worked with colored silk yarns mainly in stem and satin stitches and with couched silver and gilt yarns.

82. Rumal. Plain-weave cotton foundation worked with colored silk yarns and gilt yarns in double darning and double running stitches so that the embroidery is reversible.

84. Cushion cover or floor mat. Plain-weave cotton foundation worked with colored silk yarns in double darning stitches.

86. Prayer carpet or hanging. Pieces of plain-weave napped wool fabrics joined by rows of chain stitching worked with

silk yarns, and edged with couched gilt cords.

87. Hanging. Plain-weave linen foundation worked with colored silks in darning stitches.

88. Ornamental towel end. Plain-weave linen foundation worked with silk yarns in double running stitches and with silver and gilt tinsels.

91. Bed tent. Plain-weave linen foundation worked with colored silk yarns in cross and Rhodian step stitches.

92. Scarf or towel end. Plain-weave linen foundation worked with colored silk yarns (mainly red and violet) and silver and gilt yarns in couched, brick and stem stitches and deflected-element embroidery.

94. Fragment of a garment or hanging. Plain-weave cotton foundation worked with colored wool yarns in darning stitches.

96. Man's robe. Damask-weave cotton foundation worked with cotton or silk yarns in stem, couching, chain and eyelet stitches.

101. Woman's sleeveless shirt. Plain-weave cotton foundation with cotton and silk inlaid weaving at the top; spots of needlework within the inlaid area, using colored cotton or silk yarns in darning stitches; applications of plain-weave black silk near the neck, bordered with needlework using colored silk yarns in chain stitches.

102. Doily. Plain-weave linen foundation worked with blue and white linen yarns in Romanian, stem, feather, lattice and buttonhole stitches.

103. Part of a bedcover. Plain-weave linen foundation worked mainly in self-couching, lattice, cross and stem stitches.

105. Part of a border. Plain-weave linen foundation worked with red silk yarn mainly in cross and double running stitches.

106. Cushion cover. Plain-weave linen foundation worked with red silk yarn in darning stitches.

107. Power-woven fabric. Cotton ground, red silk pattern.

Glossary

altar dossal, hanging or structure covering the space immediately above and behind an altar; decorated with orphreys, sacred emblems or pictorial compositions.

altar frontal, hanging or structure covering the front of an altar; decorated with orphreys, sacred emblems or pictorial compositions.

applied work, needlework procedure or fabric whose ornamentation consists of pieces of colored, patterned or specially textured fabrics or other materials sewn to the surface of a foundation fabric that extends the full size of the finished piece. The pieces are shaped to create a pattern when assembled; they are arranged on the foundation either on one level or on top of one another so that the smallest pattern elements appear on the uppermost level rather than the lowest. See also *reverse applied work*.

art needlework, consciously "artistic" needlework representing a return to more elegant traditions of embroidery, which developed toward the end of the nineteenth century in England as a reaction against the mechanical, mass-produced effects of *Berlin work* and the dehumanizing of handiwork in general.

Berlin work (Berlin wool work), needlework procedure or fabric involving special wool yarns, paper patterns and canvas, originally produced in Berlin and later elsewhere as well. The pattern was transferred to the canvas by means of counted-thread work; eventually silk yarns and beads were also incorporated into the pictorial and ornamental compositions.

bobbin lace, openwork fabric created with the aid of many small bobbins, each carrying one yarn; the bobbins are manipulated in such a way as to cause their yarns to intermesh and thus construct a plaited fabric.

broadcloth, wide, heavy wool fabric with a feltlike, napped surface that hides the woven structure.

brocade (brocaded, brocading), weave in which a pattern is created in a fabric by the intersections of a supplementary warp and supplementary wefts that are different in size, color or texture from the main warp and wefts; the pattern or brocading wefts are introduced into the ground weave by hand with the aid of bobbins and do not extend across the full width of the fabric from selvedge to selvedge.

chenille, yarn with edges of short pile twisted to form a furry cord; used as a texture accent in decorative textiles.

couching, fixing a yarn to the surface of a foundation by means of small stitches made with a finer yarn that crosses the heavier (pattern) yarn; the couching stitches may be nearly invisible or arranged to form a secondary pattern or texture.

counted-thread work, needlework procedure or fabric whose pattern is created by working stitches in places determined by counting warp and weft yarns rather than by following the lines in a pattern drawn on the foundation.

crazy quilt, type of coverlet, usually not quilted, made toward the end of the nineteenth century with irregularly shaped, colored and textured bits of fabric pieced together to form the top, which was then further treated with needlework to create extraordinarily rich and often bizarre visual effects.

crewel, long-staple wool yarn used for needlework; it is loosely twisted and plied (several strands used together).

cutwork (cut-fabric work), needlework procedure or fabric using a foundation of woven material that has been cut away in places to create a pattern; stitches are used both to hold the cut yarns in place and also to add ornamental shapes and details.

damask, woven fabric with a self-pattern created on the loom by reversing the faces of a weave; for instance, showing a warp twill weave against a background of weft twill on the front of the fabric and the reverse on the back.

deflected-element embroidery, needlework procedure or openwork fabric in which the embroidery stitches are not only decorative but also pull the warp and weft yarns of the woven foundation slightly out of their original positions and thus create small open spaces in the foundation fabric.

fustian, twill-woven fabric having a linen warp, cotton wefts and a napped finish; used in Britain and North America in the seventeenth and eighteenth centuries as the foundation for much crewel embroidery.

gauze, special form of weaving in which pairs of adjacent warp yarns cross each other between rows of weft, thereby pulling the pairs closer together and separating the lines of weft; the resulting fabric has a more open texture than usual.

inlaid weaving, weave in which a pattern is created by the intersections of the warp and one or more supplementary weft yarns different in size, color or texture from the main wefts and introduced by hand, with the aid of bobbins, into the main web as it is being woven. The pattern wefts do not extend entirely across the fabric from selvedge to selvedge but wind back and forth in relatively restricted areas. Compare to *brocading*.

napping, finishing process used to raise the short fibers (usually weft fibers) to the surface of a woven fabric to form a nap or fuzzy texture.

needle painting, general term used to designate the kind of needlework that imitates painting in both design and technique, the stitches treated as though they were strokes of a paintbrush.

needlepoint lace, openwork fabric created with the aid of a needle, with or without a woven or netted foundation.

opus anglicanum, Latin term for medieval English needlework; literally, "English work."

orphrey, an ornamental band or panel usually decorated with needlework and applied to an ecclesiastical vestment or altar furnishing; panels on altar frontals, dalmatics or tunicles are also called apparels.

overshot weaving, weave in which a pattern is created by the intersections of the warp and one or more supplementary wefts different in size, color or texture from the main wefts. The pattern wefts are carried in a shuttle that is thrown across the full width of the fabric from selvedge to selvedge.

pieced work or *patchwork*, needlework fabric whose structure and ornamentation depend on the sewing together edge to edge, mosaic fashion, of pieces of fabric of the same or different weaves with a variety of colors, patterns or textures.

plain weave or *tabby weave*, weave in which each weft yarn passes over and under each warp yarn and then alternately in the next row as the weft crosses the fabric from selvedge to selvedge; the finished fabric shows a simple basket-weave surface. Also called cloth weave. See plate 27.

purl, silver, gilded metal or other metal wire, sometimes painted or wrapped with colored silk threads used as embroidery yarns, sewn to the foundation fabric.

quilt, needlework procedure or fabric involving stitches made through two layers of fabric that usually but not always have between them either a layer of wadding or a soft cord—either material serving to throw the stitched pattern into relief.

raised work, term used before the end of the nineteenth century to designate needlework executed on padded foundations, producing ornamental or pictorial compositions in relief. See also *stump work*.

resist dyeing, method of imparting a pattern to a textile by applying a resist medium—wax, paste, tightly tied string, etc.—to a fabric and then dipping it into a dye bath. Since the dye cannot penetrate the resist medium, the protected areas show the color of the original fabric when the resist medium is removed.

reverse applied work, needlework procedure or fabric whose ornamentation is produced by sewing pieces of colored, patterned or specially textured fabrics or other materials to the surface of a foundation fabric that extends the full size of the finished piece. The applied pieces are shaped to create a pattern when they are assembled, and they are arranged so that the smallest pattern elements appear on the lowest level rather than on the uppermost, as in regular applied work. Compare to *applied work*.

rug knotting, basic procedure for producing sturdy pile fabrics by tying decorative yarns in one or more kinds of looped knots on the warp as the fabric is being woven; the loops appear only on the right side of the fabric and are usually cut to form a pile.

satin weave, weave in which each weft yarn passes over or under one or more warp yarns in a regular but unequal sequence that is alternated in each row of weaving in such a way as to create a fabric with a surface of relatively long, unbroken expanses of warp or weft yarns that obscure the intersections and produce the effect of a smooth, glossy surface. See plate 27.

selvedges, the two parallel edges of any woven fabric, running the length of the piece.

stump work, a nineteenth-century term for a type of seventeenth-century English raised work revived briefly during the nineteenth century. See also *raised work*.

tapestry, woven fabric whose pattern and structure are created simultaneously by weaving weft yarns into those parts of the warp where the pattern demands a particular color. The wefts never travel from selvedge to selvedge across the full width of the fabric, and therefore a tapestry-woven fabric is in a sense a mosaic of patches of colored weft yarns held together by the lengthwise yarn—the warp.

tinsel, thin, flat, narrow strips of silver, gilded metal or other metals; used as embroidery yarns.

Turkey work, term usually, but not always, referring to a coarse-pile upholstery fabric with a pattern in many colors that is produced by rug knotting. The term also has been used to refer to an indeterminate kind of needlework that decorated handkerchiefs in the early eighteenth century.

twill weave, weave in which each weft yarn passes over or under one or more warp yarns in a regular but unequal sequence; this creates the effect of diagonal lines or ridges on the surface of the fabric in the warp or weft direction. See plate 27.

underside couching, fixing a yarn to the surface of a fabric by means of stitches that lie on the back of the foundation and pull tiny loops of the couched yarn to the back, thus rendering the couching stitches entirely invisible. See also *couching*.

velvet, fabric with a pile surface produced by introducing a supplementary warp system that is raised in loops above the foundation weave; the loops are later cut to form a furry pile or are left uncut to form a looped-pile surface. Velvets produced by a different, double-cloth method show only cut warp pile. Pile fabrics produced by using supplementary wefts rather than warp yarns are known as velveteen.

warp and *weft*, the two main structural elements in any woven fabric. The warp is the series of yarns running from the back to the front (or top to bottom) of a loom and ultimately the length of the finished fabric. The weft yarns run across the width of the warp from selvedge to selvedge.

withdrawn-element work, needlework procedure or fabric using a foundation of woven material from which some warp and/or weft yarns have been pulled out, or withdrawn; the remaining structural elements serve as a skeletal framework for decorative stitches.

Reading and Reference

Technical

DILLMONT, THÉRÈSE DE. *Encyclopedia of Needlework.* Mulhouse, France: T. de Dillmont, 1886 (and later editions by the same and other publishers).

ENTHOVEN, JACQUELINE. *The Stitches of Creative Embroidery.* New York: Reinhold Publishing Corp., 1964.

THOMAS, MARY. *Mary Thomas's Dictionary of Embroidery Stitches.* New York: William Morrow and Co., 1935.

General

ANTROBUS, MRS. GUY (MARY SYMONDS), AND LOUISA PREECE. *Needlework Through the Ages.* London: Hodder & Stoughton, 1928.

CLABBURN, PAMELA. *The Needleworker's Dictionary.* New York: William Morrow and Co., 1976. Contains extensive bibliography.

GOSTELOW, MARY. *The Complete International Book of Embroidery.* New York: Simon and Schuster, 1977. Contains extensive bibliography.

SCHUETTE, MARIE, AND SIGRID MÜLLER-CHRISTENSEN. *A Pictorial History of Embroidery.* Text translated by Donald King. New York: Frederick A. Praeger, 1964.

Particular Regions and Cultures

CABOT, NANCY. "Engravings and Embroideries: The Sources of Some Designs in the Fishing Lady Pictures." *Antiques,* December 1941, pp. 367–69.

DOCKSTADER, FREDERICK J. *Indian Art in America.* Greenwich, Conn.: New York Graphic Society, 1961.

FREEHOF, LILLIAN S., AND BUCKY KING. *Embroideries and Fabrics for Synagogue and Home.* New York: Hearthside Press, 1966.

GARRETT, ELIZABETH DONAGHY. "American Samplers and Needlework Pictures in the DAR Museum." 2 parts. Part I: 1739–1806, *Antiques,* February 1974, pp. 356–64; Part II: 1806–1840, *Antiques,* April 1975, pp. 688–701.

HARBESON, GEORGIANA BROWN. *American Needlework.* New York: Coward-McCann, 1938.

D'HARCOURT, RAOUL. *Textiles of Ancient Peru and Their Techniques.* Edited by Grace G. Denny and Carolyn M. Osborne. Translated by Sadie Brown. Seattle: University of Washington Press, 1962.

IRWIN, JOHN, AND MARGARET HALL. *Indian Embroideries.* Historic Textiles of India at the Calico Museum Series, no. 2. Ahmedabad, India: Bastikar, 1973.

JEWISH MUSEUM. *Fabric of Jewish Life: Textiles from the Jewish Museum Collection.* New York: Jewish Museum, 1977. Exhibition catalogue.

JOHNSTONE, PAULINE. *A Guide to Greek Island Embroidery.* London: Her Majesty's Stationery Office (for the Victoria and Albert Museum), 1972.

MAILEY, JEAN. *Embroidery of Imperial China.* New York: China House Gallery, China Institute of America, 1978. Exhibition catalogue.

MORRIS, BARBARA J. *Victorian Embroidery.* New York: Thomas Nelson and Sons, 1963.

NEVINSON, JOHN L. *Catalogue of English Domestic Embroidery of the Sixteenth and Seventeenth Centuries.* London: His Majesty's Stationery Office (for the Victoria and Albert Museum), 1938. Reprinted 1950.

ROWE, ANN POLLARD. "Crewel Embroidered Bed Hangings in Old and New England." *Bulletin: Museum of Fine Arts, Boston,* LXXI, nos. 365 and 366 (1973), pp. 102–63.

SAFFORD, CARLETON L., AND ROBERT BISHOP. *America's Quilts and Coverlets.* New York: E. P. Dutton and Co., 1972.

Textile Designs of Japan. 3 vols. Osaka: Japan Textile Color Design Center, 1959–61.

TOWNSEND, GERTRUDE. "Notes on New England Needlework before 1800." *Bulletin of the Needle and Bobbin Club,* XXVIII, nos. 1 and 2 (1944), pp. 3–23.

WEIR, SHELAGH. *Palestinian Embroidery: A Village Arab Craft.* London: British Museum, 1970.

Samplers

BOLTON, ETHEL S., AND EVA J. COE. *American Samplers.* Boston: Massachusetts Society of the Colonial Dames of America, 1921. Reprint, New York: Dover Publications, 1973.

HORNOR, MARIANNA MERRITT. *The Story of Samplers.* Philadelphia: Philadelphia Museum of Art, 1971.

KING, DONALD. *Samplers.* London: Her Majesty's Stationery Office (for the Victoria and Albert Museum), 1960.

Costume: Civil and Ecclesiastical

ANTROBUS, MRS. GUY (MARY SYMONDS), AND LOUISA PREECE. *Needlework in Religion.* London: Sir I. Pitman and Sons, 1924.

BOUCHER, FRANÇOIS. *20,000 Years of Fashion.* New York: Harry N. Abrams, 1967.

DAVENPORT, MILLIA. *The Book of Costume.* 2 vols. New York: Crown Publishers, 1948.

FAIRSERVIS, WALTER A. *Costumes of the East.* Riverside, Conn.: Chatham Press, 1971.

MAYER-THURMAN, CHRISTA C. *Raiment for the Lord's Service.* Chicago: Art Institute of Chicago, 1975. Exhibition catalogue.

Periodicals

Antiques; Bulletin of the Needle and Bobbin Club (New York); *CIBA Review; Embroidery: The Journal of the Embroiderers' Guild* (London). Also bulletins, catalogues, guidebooks and picture books published by art, ethnological and history museums.

Some Public Collections
of Needlework

UNITED STATES

Boston:	Museum of Fine Arts
Chicago:	The Art Institute of Chicago
Cleveland:	Cleveland Museum of Art
Detroit:	The Detroit Institute of Arts
Indianapolis:	Indianapolis Museum of Art
Los Angeles:	Los Angeles County Museum of Art
New York City:	The Brooklyn Museum
	Cooper-Hewitt Museum, the Smithsonian Institution's National Museum of Design
	The Metropolitan Museum of Art
	The Museum of the American Indian, Heye Foundation
Philadelphia:	Philadelphia Museum of Art
Richmond, Va.:	Valentine Museum
St. Louis:	The St. Louis Art Museum
Washington, D.C.:	Smithsonian Institution
	National Museum of History and Technology
	The Textile Museum
Williamsburg, Va.:	Colonial Williamsburg
Winterthur, Del.:	The Henry Francis du Pont Winterthur Museum

OTHER

Ahmedabad, India:	Calico Museum of Textiles
Amsterdam:	Rijksmuseum
Athens:	Benaki Museum
Bath, England:	Museum of Costume
Brussels:	Musées Royaux d'Art et d'Histoire
Glasgow:	Art Gallery and Museum, Burrell Collection
London:	Victoria and Albert Museum
Manchester, England:	Gallery of English Costume
Paris:	Musée des Arts Décoratifs
	Musée de Cluny
Toronto:	Royal Ontario Museum

Index

Numbers in *italics* indicate pages on which black-and-white illustrations appear. Numbers in **boldface** indicate pages on which colorplates appear.

Acknowledgments

Cooper-Hewitt staff members have been responsible for the following contributions to the series: concept, Lisa Taylor; administration, John Dobkin and Christian Rohlfing; coordination, Pamela Theodoredis. In addition, valuable help has been provided by S. Dillon Ripley, Joseph Bonsignore, Susan Hamilton and Robert W. Mason of the Smithsonian Institution, as well as by the late Warren Lynch, Gloria Norris and Edward E. Fitzgerald of Book-of-the-Month Club, Inc.

The author wishes to thank the following persons for the help and suggestions they gave him during the preparation of this book: Reiko Brandon and Sanna Deutsch, Honolulu Academy of Arts; Philip C. Gifford, American Museum of Natural History; Mary Grimes and Mary Ballard, The Detroit Institute of Arts; Donald King and Wendy Hefford, Victoria and Albert Museum; Jean Mailey, Barbara Teague, Janet S. Byrne, Mavis Dalton, Judith McGee, Gordon Stone and Elizabeth R. Usher and her staff (Watson Library), The Metropolitan Museum of Art; Larry Salmon and his staff, Department of Textiles, Museum of Fine Arts, Boston; Milton Sonday, Gillian Moss and Elaine Dee, Cooper-Hewitt Museum; Cecelia Steinfeldt, Witte Memorial Museum. He also gratefully acknowledges the help and guidance given him by Doris Bowman and Edith Standen, who read the manuscript, and by Brenda Gilchrist, Lisa Little, Gloria Norris and Joan Hoffman.

Credits

DATE DUE